Becoming an International School Educator

This resource elucidates and helps teachers navigate the international school recruitment world.

Designed for current or aspiring international school educators, this practical resource explores current issues that are relevant to the unique needs of teachers when they transition to the international school sector. Full of experience-based tips, insights, and stories from principals, curriculum coordinators, directors, school counselors, department heads, support specialists, advisors, and classroom teachers, this book explores the topics of wanderlust, English language teaching, identity and belonging, curricular standards, inclusion, diversity, and equity.

Whether you are a student or novice teacher plotting career options, a new international school hire, or an experienced educator looking for a rewarding change, this valuable resource will help you prepare as you embark on what is often considered "the best kept secret" in education.

Dana Specker Watts is the Director of Learning, Research and Outreach for International Schools Services.

Jayson W. Richardson is Professor and Department Chair of Educational Leadership and Policy Studies in the Morgridge College of Education at the University of Denver and Director of the Center for the Advanced Study in Technology Leadership (CASTLE).

Other Eye On Education Books Available from Routledge
(www.routledge.com/eyeoneducation)

Bringing Innovative Practices to Your School: Lessons from International Schools
Jayson W. Richardson

Leadership for Deeper Learning: Facilitating School Innovation and Transformation
Jayson W. Richardson, Justin Bathon, and Scott McLeod

Trailblazers for Whole School Sustainability: Case Studies of Educators in Action
Cynthia L. Merse, Jennifer Seydel, Lisa A.W. Kensler, and David Sobel

Get Organized Digitally!: The Educator's Guide to Time Management
Frank Buck

Creating, Grading, and Using Virtual Assessments: Strategies for Success in the K-12 Classroom
Kate Wolfe Maxlow, Karen L. Sanzo, and James Maxlow

Leadership in America's Best Urban Schools
Joseph F. Johnson, Jr., Cynthia L. Uline, and Lynne G. Perez

Teaching Practices from America's Best Urban Schools: A Guide for School and Classroom Leaders
Joseph F. Johnson, Jr., Cynthia L. Uline, and Lynne G. Perez

Rural America's Pathways to College and Career: Steps for Student Success and School Improvement
Rick Dalton

A Guide to Impactful Teacher Evaluations: Let's Finally Get It Right!
Joseph O. Rodgers

A Guide to Early College and Dual Enrollment Programs: Designing and Implementing Programs for Student Achievement
Russ Olwell

The Strategy Playbook for Educational Leaders: Principles and Processes
Isobel Stevenson and Jennie Weiner

Unpacking Your learning Targets: Aligning Student Learning to Standards
Sean McWherter

Strategic Talent Leadership for Educators: A Practical Toolkit
Amy A. Holcombe

Becoming a Transformative Leader: A Guide to Creating Equitable Schools
Carolyn M. Shields

Working with Students that Have Anxiety: Creative Connections and Practical Strategies
Beverley H. Johns, Donalyn Heise, Adrienne D. Hunter

Implicit Bias in Schools: A Practitioner's Guide
Gina Laura Gullo, Kelly Capatosto, and Cheryl Staats

Becoming an International School Educator

Stories, Tips, and Insights from Teachers and Leaders

Edited by
Dana Specker Watts and
Jayson W. Richardson

NEW YORK AND LONDON

Cover image: Rhys Watts (https://www.instagram.com/d.r.watts)

First published 2022
by Routledge
605 Third Avenue, New York, NY 10158

and by Routledge
4 Park Square, Milton Park, Abingdon, Oxon, OX14 4RN

Routledge is an imprint of the Taylor & Francis Group, an informa business

© 2022 selection and editorial matter, Dana Specker Watts and Jayson W. Richardson; individual chapters, the contributors

The right of Dana Specker Watts and Jayson W. Richardson to be identified as the authors of the editorial material, and of the authors for their individual chapters, has been asserted in accordance with sections 77 and 78 of the Copyright, Designs and Patents Act 1988.

All rights reserved. No part of this book may be reprinted or reproduced or utilised in any form or by any electronic, mechanical, or other means, now known or hereafter invented, including photocopying and recording, or in any information storage or retrieval system, without permission in writing from the publishers.

Trademark notice: Product or corporate names may be trademarks or registered trademarks, and are used only for identification and explanation without intent to infringe.

Library of Congress Cataloging-in-Publication Data
Names: Watts, Dana Specker, editor. | Richardson, Jayson, editor.
Title: Becoming an international school educator: stories, tips, and insights from teachers and leaders / edited by Dana Specker Watts and Jayson W. Richardson.
Description: New York, NY : Routledge, 2022. | Includes bibliographical references.
Identifiers: LCCN 2021050970 (print) | LCCN 2021050971 (ebook) |
ISBN 9780367678333 (paperback) | ISBN 9780367652630 (hardback) |
ISBN 9781003133056 (ebook)
Subjects: LCSH: Teachers, Foreign—Employment. | International education. |
Teacher exchange programs.
Classification: LCC LB2283 .B43 2022 (print) | LCC LB2283 (ebook) |
DDC 370.116—dc23/eng/20220106
LC record available at https://lccn.loc.gov/2021050970
LC ebook record available at https://lccn.loc.gov/2021050971

ISBN: 978-0-367-65263-0 (hbk)
ISBN: 978-0-367-67833-3 (pbk)
ISBN: 978-1-003-13305-6 (ebk)

DOI: 10.4324/9781003133056

Typeset in Optima
by codeMantra

Contents

Meet the Authors viii

Introduction ix

SECTION I: THE PORTABLE PROFESSION: THE WHAT AND THE WHY OF TEACHING OVERSEAS 1

1. **When Are You Going to Settle Down** 3
   Kelly Scotti

2. **Getting into International Teaching as a Student** 9
   Mick Hill

3. **The Trailing Spouse** 14
   Sally Edwards

4. **Professional Development Edventures** 19
   Jay Brownrigg

5. **Principals, Don't Wait for Retirement to Work Overseas** 25
   David Lovelin

SECTION II: A JOURNEY OF CONNECTIVISM 31

6. **My Whirlwind ESL Teaching Experience in China** 33
   Elizabeth Onayemi

7. **Building Bridges in a Globally Diverse Setting** 39
   Sandra Chow

Contents

8. **Community in the International Classroom: The Power of Storytelling** 45
Jamie Bacigalupo

9. **Belonging** 51
Tsayli Lily Chang

10. **The Healing Power of an International Community** 56
Elizabeth Heejin Cho

11. **Doing Change Well** 62
Brenda Perkins

SECTION III: CHALLENGES AND ADVERSITY WHILE TEACHING OVERSEAS **69**

12. **The Many Faces of China** 71
Ann Marie Luce

13. **Cultural Understanding in Bali** 77
Beccy Fox

14. **Culture is Complex** 82
Nicolas E. Pavlos

15. **No - I'm Not a World Language Teacher** 88
David Han

16. **One of a Few** 96
Alex Munro

17. **MacGyver Teaching, Connected Learning: Making Social Studies Learning Relevant, Uplifting and Compelling for International School Students** 101
Laura Benson

SECTION IV: MEETING THE NEEDS OF INTERNATIONAL STUDENTS: SAME SAME BUT DIFFERENT **107**

18. **A Classroom Teacher's Perspective on Special Education in International School** 109
Philip Allen

Contents

19. The Long Road to Inclusion 115
Lori Boll

20. Cultivating Community and Continuity through Learning Support 121
Erika Hardy

21. The Importance of Educating the Community about the Role of a School Counselor 127
Cheryl-Ann Weekes

22. International Counseling: A Perspective 133
Rebecca F. Stallworth

23. International Educators Touch Lives and Shape the World 139
Monika Dewan

Appendix A: Common Vocabulary Used within International Schools 145
Appendix B: International Recruiting Agencies 154
Contributor Biographies 155

Meet the Authors

Dana Specker Watts, Ph.D. is the Director of Learning, Research and Outreach for International Schools Services. She has a broad background in curriculum, technology, innovation, and educational leadership within international schools located in Hong Kong, India, and Thailand. She is also an Apple Distinguished Educator, a Google Certified Teacher, and an ISTE Certified Trainer. In addition to being an international educator, Dr. Watts has also served as Executive Director of WLead and as the Director of Innovation at 21st Century Learning International. She earned her Doctor of Philosophy in Educational Sciences from the University of Kentucky, and her current research focuses on professional development and leadership issues specific to diversity, equity, and inclusion within international schools.

Jayson W. Richardson, Ph.D. is a Professor and Department Chair of the Department of Educational Leadership and Policy Studies in the Morgridge College of Education at the University of Denver. His research is focused on exploring how school administrators lead technology-suffused, innovative learning organizations that prepare students to be future-ready for an ever-expanding digital world. Jayson is a Director of the Center for the Advanced Study in Technology Leadership (CASTLE). CASTLE is the nation's only center dedicated to the technology needs of school administrators. We also help other university educational leadership programs prepare technology-savvy school leaders and provide numerous resources for K-12 administrators and the faculty that prepare them.

Introduction

For Dana, from the moment she first considered a career in education, she dreamed of teaching overseas. For Jayson, international and intercultural education has always been the milestone of his educational career. Wanderlust has always been a part of their DNA. For both of us, we didn't know where to start, what it might entail, nor if it was possible. What we learned over our careers is that there are multitudes of ways to engage with overseas teaching. However, teaching internationally is often considered the best kept secret in education. We are here to tell you that it shouldn't be. In this book, we share stories of the how and the why of teaching in international schools.

The term 'international school' is vague and has been applied loosely within the international school community for the past few decades. The international school community is composed of private, semi-autonomous schools that pride themselves on their reputations and their ability to draw in expatriates from across the world. These broad contexts may be the main commonality that holds these organizations together.

This confusion with defining the term 'international schools' stems from the lack of homogeneity among international schools. According to The International Educator (TIE Online), an international school can be defined by having some of the following characteristics: International curriculum; multinational and multilingual student body; transferability to other international schools; international accreditation; transient and multinational teacher population; and/or a curriculum taught in English (Nagrath, 2011).

Introduction

Defining an international school can also be problematic due to different regulations and laws throughout the world which has created a cross-pollination of some international schools into multiple models. Breaking down international schools into defined categories can be even more challenging. International schools are sometimes classified into a hierarchy or tier system which may be influenced by certification, accreditation, location and region, IB/AP, national curriculum, and size. To better understand the common vocabulary of international schools, see Appendix B.

According to internal data from ISC Research (2021), as of September 2021, there were 12,535 international schools with an additional 385 schools in development. These schools employ 662,000 educators who serve 6.9 million students. Since 2011, the growth of international schools has been about 60% for the number of schools, the number of students, and the number of employed educators. These schools collectively bring in $53 USD billion in student fees.

An international teacher is often defined as an educator associated with providing a "global, intercultural, multinational and multicultural education" (Thompson, 2002, cited in Risch, 2008, p. 5). International teachers are generally certified, local or overseas hires, contracted to provide an international curriculum to multinational students usually for a minimum of two years.

The demographics associated with the international schools can vary within the teachers and students. Children of expatriates may come from above-average socioeconomic backgrounds, whose parents are employed by government agencies, international corporations, embassies, and other non-government and government institutions (Risch, 2008). This multinational student body is unique in its ability to integrate the knowledge

Table 0.1 Number of international schools

Americas	1,558
Africa	1,373
Asia	7,178
Europe	2,324
Oceana	102
Total	**12,535**

Note: Data retrieved from ISC Research (2021) internal database.

base and challenging curriculum from a multitude of countries around the world. Admission to the international schools is dependent on each school model and the bylaws of each individual school. While the primary market for international schools was initially expatriate students, Brummit and Keeling (2013) found an increase in local students applying to international schools, which has a significant impact on the current student demographic.

When you step into the world of international teaching, you will meet colleagues from different backgrounds and varied beliefs in pedagogy and instructional design. You will meet students with a wealth of experiences who have lived through extraordinary circumstances, oftentimes in cities you never heard of. As an international educator, you will be provided opportunities to grow professionally and still travel to parts of the world you previously could not locate on a map.

A frequent question that expat educators are asked is how many languages do you know? Or were all of your students from the host country? And what were your living conditions like? These are all valid questions, and we have asked educators from around the globe to share their stories with you to get at those questions.

As the past several years of living through the Covid pandemic have constantly reminded us, our world is much smaller and interconnected than our predecessors ever imagined. Zoom calls, social media connections, and a globally connected supply chain allow us to stay connected in new innovative ways every day. The power of connectivism has never been stronger. But who is working to teach the students of tomorrow? The answer is, these individuals are some of the most phenomenal educators from around the world who choose to live in countries outside their home and educate students who are often not from their home culture. Each year they face new challenges and live in a world filled with uncertainty, uprooting, and transition. We envisioned this book as a way to share some of the powerful stories and experiences of just a handful of these educators.

Within these pages, you will find tales of how educators found themselves teaching overseas. You will hear stories of the search for belonging in a new community. You will learn about adversities and challenges that teachers faced while immersed in new cultures. You will feel the compassion and love of students from around the world. Come join us on a journey into teaching overseas – the best kept secret in education.

Introduction

 ## How This Book Is Organized

This book focuses on educators' experiences within international schools. Rather than reporting on studies, we attempted to capture the lived experiences of teachers and school leaders within this unique context. The nationalities of the authors in this book are diverse, as are the schools in which they teach and lead. As such, these educators are teaching in a third culture and masterfully walk the reader through what that experience has been like for them. Contributors include principals, curriculum coordinators, directors, school counselors, department heads, support specialists, advisors, and of course, classroom teachers. As such, the reader of this book will be presented with a broad swath of stories that highlight the experiences of becoming an expatriate educator.

This book is organized into four sections. Section 1 is titled *The Portable Profession: The What and the Why of Teaching Overseas*. This section contains five chapters where each author presents a different answer to what it means to be an international educator and why they became one. Section 2 is titled *A Journey of Connectivism*. This section contains five chapters as well. Authors of these chapters discuss the connections and connectedness of living overseas and working in international schools. Section 3 focuses on acclimating into the new life of an international educator. Titled *Challenges and Adversity While Teaching Overseas*, this section contains five chapters. The fourth and final section is titled *Same Same But Different: Meeting the Needs of International Students*. In six chapters authors share stories about how being an international educator has similarities yet stark differences to what one may be used to in a more traditional setting.

 ## Who Is This Book for?

The prime audience of the book is any educator who is thinking about finding a position in an international school. This book would be useful for student teachers and novice teachers who are plotting their career options. Additionally this book can be a valuable resource for new international school hires as they begin to navigate their journey overseas to their new school. This book might also be useful to the experienced educator who is looking for a rewarding change. Heads of schools can use this book as a resource for their new faculty to better prepare for the cultural adaptations that are on the horizon.

So Are You Ready to Learn More....

Entering the world of international schools can be daunting to say the least. To start, educators might want to begin by registering with an established recruiting agency. Recruiting agencies can help provide educators guidance as they navigate the multiple options available when it comes to teaching overseas. International schools actively recruit certified educators each year to fill positions within their schools due to their transient population. These positions can be highly sought after by educators throughout the world due to benefits, salary, and the opportunity to engage in developing an international global curriculum.

The recruiting season traditionally begins at the start of the academic year, sometimes as early as August or September for the following school year and may continue into April and May. Faculty are generally required within the first few months of the school year to sign a contract which states their intention to remain at the school or search elsewhere. This process jumpstarts the recruiting season, with school leaders searching to find other teachers to fill those upcoming vacancies for the upcoming year. Due to the issues with passports, visas, housing, and other needs, this entails a long process for international schools.

For educators who are new to international schools, contracts generally require a two-year commitment which may include housing, tuition for dependents, and travel back and forth to their home country (country of origin or passport country). The interview process is also incredibly unique compared to traditional interview practices. For example during an interview, a candidate may be asked to disclose their marriage status, the number of dependents they have and their ages, their religion, the origin of their passport, and spoken languages. A reputable recruiting agency can help candidates navigate which questions are appropriate, help candidates acquire the needed paperwork including background checks, and provide access to reputable schools. These details may seem obtrusive; however, these schools often need to know this information to assess whether they can employ an individual and get them the proper visa in the host country. For example, some countries will only allow one dependent per visa, so if a family has three dependents, one child will not be able to get a visa and be unable to accompany their parents to the new post. Additionally some schools actively seek teaching couples to fill two positions within their school, whereas some schools search for individuals to fill positions and do not want the extra burden of finding a position for a spouse within their school. Furthermore, some schools may be associated with a religious organization and answer to an outside entity regarding the mission of their school. In some countries, it can be very difficult to obtain a visa depending on a person's passport. Recently there has been a strong push within the international sector to eliminate the term 'native language' from job applications to help eliminate the discrimination of non-Western educators within international schools. Although the use of the term 'native language' is becoming less common, it is still prevalent within the search process. To find out more about recruiting agencies, please see Appendix B.

References

Brummitt, N., & Keeling, A. (2013). Charting the growth of international schools. In R. Pearce (Ed.), *International education and schools: Moving beyond the first 40 years* (pp. 25–37). Bloomsbury.

ISC Research. (2021, September 17). *Live market data*. ISC Research Portal. Retrieved September 17, 2021, from https://portal.iscresearch.com/.

Nagrath, C. (2011, August 26). What makes a school international? *The International Educator (TIE Online)*. Retrieved September 16, 2021, from https://www.tieonline.com/article/87/what-makes-a-school-international-.

Risch, R. P. (2008). *On the move: Transition programs in international schools* [Unpublished doctoral dissertation]. Lehigh University.

SECTION 1

The Portable Profession
The What and the Why of Teaching Overseas

Teaching overseas may be one of the most portable careers for those with wanderlust. There are multiple entry points for anyone looking to teach within the international schools. The need for education and teachers who are passionate about the students they teach is universal. The need for teachers is constantly growing throughout the world. According to ISC Research (2021) internal data, the number of educators teaching overseas has grown from 328,661 to 550,846 over the past ten years (2011–2021). As new international schools continue to open, and the world becomes more globally connected, the need for quality teachers will only continue. International school teaching is the portable profession that allows folks to explore the world as they share their passion for education with others.

This first section of this book focuses on the portability of being an international school education. Section 1 begins with a chapter titled "When Are You Going to Settle Down" written by Kelly Scotti. In this chapter, Kelly explores the privileges and price of living overseas as an educator and the age-old question of when and how to settle down and plant roots somewhere in the world. In Mick Hill's chapter, he focuses on "Getting into International Teaching as a Student" where he shares his journey of getting into international teaching. Chapter 3 is titled "The Trailing Spouse." Here, Sally Edwards shares stories of having a career in education while following

DOI: 10.4324/9781003133056-1

her spouse around the world. Sally discusses the nuances of teaching and the invaluable experiences her children had while she was working as an international educator. Next, Jay Brownrigg's chapter titled "Professional Development Edventures," focuses on the professional development opportunities and the many adventures he has engaged in around the world whilst also developing and topping up his own skillset. Next David Lovelin focuses on leadership within international schools. In his chapter titled, "Principals, Don't Wait for Retirement to Work Overseas," David shares his journey from being a principal in a public school in Oregon to arriving in Korea and serving as a principal at some of the largest international schools in Asia.

In this section, these authors shared their passion for education, and how they have merged this with a never-ending sense of wanderlust. Each story and journey into international teaching is unique. Join our authors as they share snapshots of their journey into the world of international schools.

Reference

ISC Research. (2021, September 17). *Live market data*. ISC Research Portal. Retrieved September 17, 2021, from https://portal.iscresearch.com/.

When Are You Going to Settle Down?

Kelly Scotti

I come from a family of immigrants, people not afraid to venture into the world to find a better life for themselves and their families. My parents and grandparents emigrated from Belfast, Northern Ireland in the early '60s and filled our heads with stories of home, the magical place where they were raised. Nothing tasted as good as at home, people weren't as polite as at home, and scandalous things that happened in the news would never have happened at home. My siblings and I would often wonder why they never just went home to live if it was so much better.

When I left Canada to teach internationally I was 33 years old. I had eight years of teaching under my belt and I was fully vested in my pension. I worked in a purpose-built school with professional colleagues and high-achieving students. For all intents and purposes, I was following my passion. However, I had also been involved in two work-to-rule actions, one province-wide teacher strike, and my salary was frozen for five years. I stood before 35 grade 12 students preparing them for university, all the while watching marking levels rise and preparation time fall. Teaching students was no longer my focus. Trying to survive mentally and emotionally was all I could muster. While colleagues were feeling similarly, I was determined not to settle into a career that could not bring me the joy I knew teaching could be. This was not what I had signed up for and I knew drastic measures were needed to survive working in the education sector.

So I found myself, after having been raised in one of the most liveable countries in the world, leaving home to search for a better life. I wasn't fleeing my family, I wasn't running from unrequited love, and it certainly wasn't easy leaving the freedom and beauty of Canada. My career was the

DOI: 10.4324/9781003133056-2

The Portable Profession

problem. A career I loved more than anything else in the world. A career that I had pursued relentlessly throughout my studies; a career that defined me. Being an educator was my passion, and if I couldn't do it in Canada, I would need to find somewhere I could.

I answered an ad in a Toronto newspaper for an English language teaching position in Asia in March. By August, I had landed at Hong Kong International Airport to start my first overseas teaching post. A leave of absence from my position in Canada would last for two years, at which time, I naively thought, I'd reassess where I was in my life. But that's not what happened. Instead, I fell in love with teaching again, I fell in love with a German who would become my husband, and I fell in love with something I hadn't even known existed the previous year – the world of international education. No reassessment needed to happen. I'd found my passion again and I was on my way to a better life.

Today, I sit and overlook my lush garden in a suburb of Johannesburg, South Africa, and I ask myself, "how did I get here?", "What have I gained and what have I given up to live the life of an international teacher?"

These are not uncommon questions as I have asked them many times over the last 22 years: in Germany, while sipping a cold beer at a local Biergarten; while phoning into family gatherings from a beach in Thailand; while walking along a dusty road in the morning heat of Cambodia; as I drank champagne at a Michelin star restaurant on the iconic Shanghai Bund. While I have had the privilege of seeing the world up close, there was a price to pay.

Being an international teacher has made me a quintessential lifelong learner. I have reinvented the type of teacher I am, the courses I can teach, the responsibilities I take on, my response to students and their needs – with every new country and new school I join. The diversity of students and colleagues in international schools provides a rich dynamic environment that has enhanced me personally and professionally. My introduction to new languages, new customs, new ways of doing and being has allowed me to grow in ways I could not have imagined before this journey. My teaching continues to grow with every new school and community. Each year can be filled with unfamiliar students, fresh curriculum innovations, new administration, a new role, and different colleagues. Professional learning opportunities have taken me across the globe building a network of like-minded professionals from every kind of school imaginable. All the while I have sharpened my skills, opened myself to new practices, and have fully engaged in the profession. I can move between national and international curriculum models, between diverse classroom demographics and homogenous ones, and between very large and rather tiny schools. While I appear to do this seamlessly, it's not seamless. I have learned to make decisions that must consider my children, my partner, and my professional ambitions and compromises are a part of the process. My decisions have not always taken me where I thought, but they have taken me to where I needed to be and I have always grown as a result. Leaning into the professional challenges this lifestyle has presented to me has made me a better practitioner, a better collaborator, and a better leader. This is the better life I went looking for.

Being an international teacher has meant a family life that differs from that of my first family. Every trip home my mother would ask, "When are you going to settle down"? What she meant was, when are you going to buy a house, have children, live the life I had been raised in, and do what she and my father had done? But like she and my father, and my grandparents before them, I wanted something more than was on offer where I was. I knew that settling down would be different for me and my family. As an international teacher, I have found out just how wonderfully different and how heart-wrenchingly difficult it can be.

My kids don't know their grandparents the way I knew mine. They don't have sleepovers or get spoiled by *oma* and *opa*. I can't drop them at my brother's in an emergency. I can't ask my sister to babysit to have dinner alone with my husband. My kids don't really know their cousins or any extended family for that matter. I couldn't call my mom to ask for advice about something I was cooking as she'd be in bed, asleep, in another time zone. My dad can't just pop over to help me paint a room or fix a toilet. I can't stop by to have coffee with my dad in the middle of the week. I couldn't take my mom to her doctor appointments, or sit with her while she and my dad waited for test results.

My grandmother's funeral happened while we were on the beach in the South China Sea. I was too far away to make it home. The last time I hugged my mom was three months before she died, a Christmas trip to Canada decided at the last minute. These are the realities of living internationally.

Our home is where we are together, our family is those we gather close, and our support network is a group of like-minded nomads whom we may never see again after our time together. Colleagues and community members have become my friends, my confidants, my pseudo-family while my connections to the people I left behind have waned. While I may long for old friends and the comfort of what I know, trips home can be stressful. I have changed with every new move, and many friends at home have stayed the same. My life seems exotic, hectic, full of adventure to them. Some resent that and have distanced themselves from me as a result. Others act as if I saw them last week, and are not interested in the life I live when I am not there. True friends, however, still want to know every last detail. They support my life choices and my next move, no matter how remote it seems to them. They live vicariously through my adventures and our friendship continues to grow as a result.

Our family traditions are less rooted in place and more rooted in shared memories of Angkor Wat at sunrise, of Christmas with friends in Ho Chi Minh, or of whale watching at the southern tip of Africa. Home has become where we are together, the people we choose to surround ourselves with, and the shared experience of being long-term visitors in different world cultures. My children are multilingual, more at home in an airport than a shopping mall, and need two hands to count the number of bedrooms they have had in their short lives. This is the only life they know; it is their understanding of home and they are happy.

Being an international teacher can mean a career trajectory is not a smooth uphill climb, but rather filled with unimagined dips and turns. I have got jobs from attending job fairs, others through email contact with a school, and some have come from visiting a school after I've moved to a new country. Sometimes it is easy, sometimes it's not.

Navigating the international school world with a partner who is not in education has not always been ideal. Making decisions about leaving one country for another, one community for another, one school or position for another has not always been my decision alone. The timing of moves in the business world is never ideal, and school options have not always been abundant in my new location. I have, more than once, found myself teaching a grade or subject unfamiliar to me because I am a teacher and I was available. I have found myself passed up for a promotion due to a sudden move on the part of my partner. And I have found myself explaining why my CV shows a constant shifting between leadership and classroom roles. I am, however, first and foremost a teacher of children and the sacrifices and compromises have all been worth the pursuit of this passion.

The move to a new school, a new city, a new country, never ceases to excite me. It always takes me back to that first move 23 years ago. I never want to leave where I am, but I always want to move on to the next adventure, the next culture, the next school. It's a fresh start, again. Uncertainty, however, is always a given. Will the children settle in the new school, will I fit into the professional culture, can we bring the dog? As my children age, these uncertainties add a level of stress that needs to be managed. Sometimes a move hasn't worked out for any number of reasons. When it didn't, I made sure to move on.

It is hard for me to imagine what my life would have been like if I had not taken that first opportunity in Asia. Now I have had a rich career of passionate work of which I am proud. I have a husband and children with whom I share this adventure. I have friends and colleagues in every time zone whose comfort and support I can always count on. I am happy, I am loved, and I am settled.

How different a person and educator am I to those colleagues who stayed behind in that small southwestern town?

When I'm home and we meet, our talk now turns to retirement. They plan to travel and see world heritage sites, maybe learn a new language. They can also recite the last day, hour, and minute they will spend in their school. I listen and smile. I've seen the world, I speak three languages, and I don't ever want to retire. I don't want to stop working with young people, I don't want to stop learning, and I don't want to leave international education. I know for certain our experiences have been different and for that I am grateful.

Canada is my home and everything is better there – the people, the weather, the food, and everyone is so polite. But I'm not going back anytime soon, I'm too settled in the rest of the world.

Advice for Others

Make the most of the time you spend in each country. Oftentimes we get caught up in the everyday life of the school and we forget about the world outside its walls. Travel within your new country, participate in cultural events, eat the food, and visit its heritage sites.

Make friends with people from your host country. This will be the best professional learning you will experience and will create memories you will take with you when you move on. Take lessons in the language of the host country, this will help you to settle and will give your own children much-needed tools for navigating the city, their neighborhood, and the clubs they may join.

Teach your children about their home country. Tell them what school was like for you, tell them of your childhood adventures no matter how small they may seem. This will teach them that there is more than one way of living and thriving in the world. Visit your home so your children can establish relationships with your extended family members. This is also a good opportunity for some alone time while they visit with grandparents, aunts and uncles, and cousins.

Stay connected to colleagues you befriend in each school. They will become your international family and you will share important milestones and events with them along your journey. They will show up again; at a job fair, while vacationing in Japan, or as a reference for someone you may be hiring in the future. These connections will help to ground you in a seemingly unstable adventure, even if only across Zoom or WhatsApp.

Always have an updated CV on your computer. Things can change pretty quickly in this world and you never know when it'll be time to start your research all over again.

Getting into International Teaching as a Student

Mick Hill

During my career, I taught in six different schools located in The Netherlands, Germany, Luxembourg, England, and Japan. These were schools following the International Baccalaureate, a German State Curriculum (Baden-Wurttemberg), the International Primary Curriculum, The Dutch National curriculum, and the National Curriculum of England and Wales. My first experience with teaching was as a class assistant for children aged four to six. This position was part of my previous education in assistant nursing. As a 16-year-old boy, it was something I was not looking forward to. I remember thinking to myself that it would be an annoying year full of screaming children. However, I was proven wrong. Within two weeks, I found my passion for teaching. I loved early childhood education. The imagination, creativity, and playfulness of the children was a unique experience. I enjoy working with people, and to work with tiny humans is fantastic and a tremendous amount of fun. I changed my career to become an early childhood educator.

My first step into international education was a spur-of-the-moment decision. I just changed career paths but did not expect international teaching to be so different from my home country. Before applying to the regular Dutch teaching program, my mother read in the local newspaper about a newly opened university program close to our home specifically focused on international education. She thought it would interest me due to my dual language proficiency. I went to their website and read the first page of the website, which said something along the lines of *"Do you love to travel, teaching and do you want to do an English education?"* After reading those words, I was sold. I immediately applied.

DOI: 10.4324/9781003133056-3

In my first year of studies, we were taught the curricular differences and practicalities among international schools. Specifically, we focused on the International Baccalaureate, International Primary Curriculum, and the National Curriculum of England and Wales. We also learned how certain countries have habits in the classroom that might differ from each student's home country. One of the most apparent and more visible differences would be the focus on teacher and student-based learning. These lessons taught me a lot about the schools in which I would soon be working. It only started to make more sense when my practical placements started.

There is a nine-week time slot allocated for a practicum placement each year during this teacher training program. My first practicum experience was at an international school in Luxembourg City, Luxembourg. This was a big school with three classes per year group. The school had a diverse student body with students who lived through and experienced a mixture of experiences and multiple schools. The school used the national curriculum for England and Wales. Until a month before my teaching practice, I never realized that there could be such a difference between different curricula. Seeing a school that worked so different from what I was used to in The Netherlands was an eye-opener. For example, the students had more subjects than my experiences as a student in The Netherlands, where we didn't have much access to the sciences. Whereas in this international school the students engaged in science nearly every day as well as regular practical IT lessons, learning about all the features of the Microsoft Office products.

Another difference between my personal experience as a primary student compared to international students was the importance of learning and that the students would help each other when there was a problem. This was not how I experienced a national curriculum as a primary student and an educational classroom assistant. Perhaps the biggest realization I had was when two fellow student teachers and I hosted a school-wide assembly. We discussed languages, and at the end of the assembly, we asked the students how many languages each of them spoke. Most of the students from this international school spoke three or more languages, and one student shared that she spoke eight. The experiences of these students opened my eyes to the diversity of the student body and community at international schools.

International Teaching as a Student

My second-year placement was at a school in Japan that was very different from those I had experienced before. For example, it is common and polite in Asian countries to take your shoes off before entering someone's home or a temple. The school also had this principle in mind and used a system of inside and outside shoes. The students would come in, change their shoes and then continue to class, and when going outside for playtime they would switch their shoes again and head out to play. Even experiencing something as innocuous as this custom made it clear to me how different we are and how different our students can be.

While in Japan, I experienced some struggles with the language. I was placed in an early childhood class with students aged three to five. Although most of the children were close to being fluent in English, a couple of students struggled to speak English, creating some challenges in this placement. Even though I cannot speak Japanese, usually, this was not a problem because the teachers and teaching assistant helped when I taught lessons.

During playtime, I observed and interacted with students, bringing understanding to what the students would mean. For instance, one of the boys couldn't speak English but he could understand it. During playtime, he would build aeroplanes of different sorts. And after building these aeroplanes, he would run up to me and yell "Sensei! Sensei!" and I would turn to him, and he would tell me something in Japanese. I then asked him if he built that aeroplane and said it was very pretty. Content, he would run away again and keep playing. It was the little moments like these of good understanding that fostered a rich and valuable experience.

Although the differences between cultures and educational styles in Europe were visible, it was all still somewhat similar. Going to Japan was an experience showing me that there were many cultural differences between our cultures. There is a very egocentric culture growing up in The Netherlands; whereas in Japan, it is more socio-centric. I found this quite refreshing and pleasant. A good example would be travelling by train. Japan is famous for the trains never being late, wherein The Netherlands trains are hardly ever on time. Getting out of a train in The Netherlands can be challenging since people try to get in there indirectly, in Japan, people wait next to the doors so people can get out first before they go inside.

By choosing this college preparation route specified for international teachers, a lot of the struggles one might find jumping into international teaching are taken away. We got eased into the experience and the differences were highlighted and explained. Going to a new country and living in different cultures will be challenging and is not something one might easily prepare for. However, the stress of a new school environment was significantly lowered due to the clear expectations that were set during the study program.

The program I followed has a clear set-out focus for the students. Although the program is relatively new, I believe I was in the sixth year group to join the program. The first two years are now focused on general teaching development by improving English proficiency, teaching practice, mathematics, educational studies lessons, and more. Following the students will pick two specializations, of which one is at a foreign/ different university to gain more international experiences. So far, the only downside to the program is that the graduates will not be receiving a teaching qualification, only a bachelor's in education. I have been told that for most job applications, this shouldn't be an issue. Most of the students that came before me got hired directly after graduation. However, I know that not every school will and some students are looking into postgraduate programs to acquire this.

Personally, I think we were prepared enough to teach classes. The bachelor's does a great job preparing you for teaching your own classes. With the biggest teaching moments being the teaching practices, gaining a lot of real-life experience. The third- and fourth-year practices build up a solid foundation, with 80% and a 100% minimum teaching time for the last two weeks, respectively.

Advice for Others

Being a student-teacher allowed me to experience international schools with less pressure than the responsibility of being a teacher and having responsibility for a class. The experiences I have gained during my studies are invaluable to me. If you are interested in becoming a teacher in international schools, the International Teacher Education program for primary schools (ITEps) can be the right start for you. This program trains a high level of English and all the skills one expects to learn from a teacher education program, as well as extra knowledge regarding international settings such as the different curricula and cultural customs.

It is however essential you are aware of your goals and aspirations. If you know where you want to work in the future, check if the qualification you would get with this program, or a similar one, would be enough for the place or country you want to go to work. Some schools prefer or are legally required to hold higher standards than others so what will be enough for one might not be up to standard for the next. It is crucial to be aware of this.

Choosing to become a teacher should be considered for the flexible working environment, working with children, and many others. Choosing to become an international teacher brings along a bigger challenge, for instance by having to adapt more to a different environment, cultural differences, and language barriers. It also brings along more opportunities for travel, to get to know different people, and to engage in different perspectives.

The Trailing Spouse
Sally Edwards

I have been a trailing spouse for 30 years. With my husband initially studying abroad and then working in international companies, every time he got a new job we moved. With the regularity of a Swiss watch the movers would turn up, box our stuff, and we would relocate somewhere in Europe. When he eventually got a job at the European Space Agency, we settled in The Netherlands where we have been for 15 years. This was our last move, and I am delighted!

As the trailing spouse in the relationship, each relocation raised the same questions. Would I be able to work? What would I do with all the time I had? Could I earn my own money? What about the local language? How could I carve out a life for myself that was separate to my husband's and not dependent on his income?

I have a Bachelor of Arts in English literature, a teaching qualification, a Master's in Business Administration (MBA), plus certificates for coaching, nonviolent communication, and first aid, whilst also speaking several European languages. Despite being well qualified, I never felt that I had a fully professional career before we settled in The Netherlands. It seems that I am not alone in this experience. Coffee mornings spent with other trailing spouses show me that they are usually also well qualified yet seem to struggle to find work when they move. One of the first questions is, "how many of you are working?"

Despite having chosen this life, the reality of living it was sometimes harder than I had imagined. The practicalities of starting my life again in another country and trying to create our life from scratch each time the movers came was always tough. I wanted to work, make my own money,

DOI: 10.4324/9781003133056-4

The Trailing Spouse

and have my own identity. This was hard to do when we were moving every three years.

When we made our final move to The Netherlands and had children, the question of schooling became important. Now, with children of our own, issues about whether to choose a local school in Dutch or an international school became more critical. As we discussed the options for our own children's education, my new career opened up. After years of trailing behind my husband I finally found a way to define my own life. I transformed from being a full-time stay-at-home mum to being a teacher, entrepreneur, writer, and contributor to the local economy. It all started with a seemingly small, inconspicuous step.

My first teaching job in The Netherlands arrived through a number of bizarre moves that seem surreal now I think about it. Someone knew someone, who knew someone who told me about a job. Eventually an email landed on my desk that included a photocopy of an advert that had been hanging up on a wall at the Space Agency. Networking is important in the expat community, and information is often passed on through informal networks of behind-the-scenes connections. With a simple phone call I landed an interview for a job as an English teacher. The school director was uncomfortable about speaking to me in English and we had a stilted conversation with my bad Dutch not really being up to scratch for doing an interview. To this day she says that she was most impressed by my accent and wanted the children to learn to speak English properly. Despite having no experience teaching at a Montessori school, they hired me.

Over the past 13 years, my understanding of the Montessori approach has deepened. The job has grown. When I started, the school used an old fashioned, boring English book. Under my guidance, English lessons became more Montessori led as the children could choose more and more of the work they did, how they learnt and what their work should look like. Now I teach nearly half of the children at the school and what started out as a little job for half a day each week has increased to two full days of teaching, with the safety of being on contract and the pension benefits that brings. Not only did I get a job I found a way of integrating into the community and changing my life.

This initial move into the working world had its challenges. My own children were at a different school in another town and my husband travelled a lot for his job. There were many weeks when I was essentially a

The Portable Profession

single mum in a foreign country with no back up from family or friends. I remember one evening I needed to be at school to do parent evenings but had no babysitter. In the end I took my children with me, sandwiches in boxes for their tea, and let them play in a classroom with the TV on, hoping they would be good. These sorts of moments reflect the downside of expat life which can sometimes be lonely and hard work. I often felt that I was constantly juggling competing demands for my energy and attention. The impact of managing work and children without help often seems to be an issue that is overlooked when considering an overseas move. Yet there is a silver lining to the story. I learned how to quickly build a support network, find out about local expat groups, and to ask for help. In doing this I settled into the local community more quickly, found friends, and started to feel at home.

My experiences over the years have combined to create a personal strength that comes from having to cope with what life throws at me. I have become adept at finding answers to questions that would be easy to deal with in my home country and mother tongue. Yet doing apparently simple things, such as connecting to the gas supply, finding an internet provider, or getting a reliable handyman can be surprisingly challenging in a foreign country! It is also incredibly rewarding when it all works out and we finally have an internet connection that works and can watch our favorite shows on BBC.

The great thing about working in an international school environment is that the school is already an expat hub. The teachers and parents are all far from home, missing their support network, and wanting to build connections and friendships as well. This makes it easier to meet other people and to find out information to help you settle in. I find that the communities in international schools are also aware of the impact on personal and family life that frequent moving has. They too are used to making friends quickly and the people in these communities seem more open to newcomers than the host country might be.

We are very blessed to have raised our children in The Netherlands, which is famous for its good work/life balance. In their primary school years my children were home on Wednesday and Friday afternoons and so was I. This gave us more time to do sports activities, meet with friends, and generally enjoy all that is on offer. Family life is important here, and we always felt the shorter school hours and generous holiday allowance supported us as a family, enabled us to be together, and provided time to explore our surroundings.

The Trailing Spouse

My children quickly learned to go everywhere by bike. The very safe cycling conditions here gave them an early independence and self-confidence that I appreciate now. As their Dutch counterparts cycled off to their football or hockey training sessions, my children joined them, shaking off my uncertainty, shouting over their shoulder as they pedaled away, "mum, everyone here goes by themselves, don't worry." We also made sure they were strong swimmers and could ice skate. We wanted them to be able to join in when the weather was cold and everyone was out on the canals skating – which is about as Dutch as you can get.

When I ask my children if they feel particularly English, they always reply with, "no." When pressed they say that they do not feel very Dutch either but see themselves as hybrid European. They speak English, Dutch, German, and a smattering of French and Spanish. Their friends come from all over the world. This has helped them become more open minded towards other cultures, languages, and people. This multi-cultural upbringing has given them a good start in life. My children have had invaluable life experiences from living here, and I do not regret our choice to stay in The Netherlands.

I found that once I got my first teaching job more and more work opportunities opened up. I no longer had to play the role of the passive trailing spouse and developed a patchwork career mixed between working on contract and being self-employed.

Now I can mostly decide when I work, what I earn, and when I have free time. My working week is flexible, I take time off when I need it and can adapt my hours to other projects I am working on. I am at home during the holidays. My working day finishes more or less at the same time as my kids, so I am at home when they are at home. International teaching has given me more flexibility and ease in managing my whole life than I ever imagined. When I combine these factors with the quality of life in The Netherlands, the easy access to the beach, and high standard of living, this has been a good move for us and my accidental career in teaching has been a bonus.

As I look back over my working life, I am amazed that I did not realize more quickly that I could get work as a teacher. It is an almost perfect portable profession. I love teaching, I love seeing children understand new things, and know that I had a helping hand in that process. As trailing spouses whose life experience is to move to different countries, why not make the best of it? We bring our experience, accumulated cultural, educational, and teaching expertise with us each time we move, and this adds up to something valuable. Why not bring all that into classrooms round the world as we move?

Advice for Others

I wish I had known earlier that there were quite a lot of flexible routes open to getting qualified to be a teacher. Even if you are not currently qualified to teach, the shortage of teachers around the world is driving training organizations to be more flexible and creative in how people can study to get qualified.

If you are interested in teaching English, the market for English teachers is massive. Work is available at professional language schools such as Linguarama, Berlitz, or the British Council. Alternatively, local primary schools in your country of residence may need English teachers, and often love to have a native English speaker at school. International schools, such as The British or American Schools have English teaching departments that help children who come from non-English speaking countries cope with the transition.

You could check out the jobs in your area if you are already living overseas. If you have not yet decided where you might like to move, the *Times Educational Supplement* lists an impressive range of job vacancies online.

An alternative method to find work is to approach schools directly. It has always worked well for me, and this helps you to gauge the job market in a particular subject area. Even if there are no vacancies, you can offer to give a workshop or a talk which can open doors.

If you are not sure that teaching is for you, why not try doing a few days' work placement, see what it feels like to be in the classroom and whether this is something for you? It is probably wise to take this precautionary step before investing in a teacher training course that might eventually lead you to realize that teaching is not your dream job after all!

Finally, it is worthwhile talking to teachers who are already working in international schools. A quick Google search can lead you to blogs and a range of social media in which teachers share their experiences of their jobs and life in their host country.

Professional Development Edventures

Jay Brownrigg

My journey into educational professional development started back in 2005 when I graduated from Edith Cowan University in Perth, Australia. Back in those days, professional development was very different from what it is today. My first memory of it was sitting in the library of the school I was teaching at and someone was talking to the staff about mathematical strategies for elementary students. At the time it meant not too much to me as I was a physical education teacher and math had nothing to do with what I teach. Oh, how I would be so wrong in the years to come. Over the next few years in Australia, I would attend a few physical education-based professional development opportunities which were amazing and I still refer to skills and activities I learned from those days today. My understanding and appreciation of professional development would start in my first year of teaching overseas in 2010. To this day I am still learning.

In August of 2010, I boarded a flight from Perth, Australia to Shanghai, China. This would be my first teaching experience overseas and I was also looking forward to starting my International Baccalaureate (IB) journey. Professional development started off the same as back in Australia. All staff got together before the school year started and the school leadership team ran a series of workshops on the introduction to the Primary Years Programme. I remember sitting in the staffroom thinking 'this stuff is just like in Australia' and also 'man I drank too much last night.' Whilst my brain was thinking about many other things like home, family, and where can I find some normal food, it didn't soak in too much.

At the beginning of 2011, I was asked to participate in physical education professional development but this was different from what I had

DOI: 10.4324/9781003133056-5

The Portable Profession

done in Australia. Back home, I participated in many physical education professional development sessions with the Australian Football League and Cricket Australia but these always involved learning about specific games or sports that we could play and do with our students. The professional development I was about to participate in had me taking a plane from China all the way to Memphis, Tennessee in the United States. It was an IB Americas conference and I was a participant in the Introduction to physical education in the Middle Years Programme (MYP). I couldn't believe it. I was about to fly halfway around the world for professional development and my school was going to pay for the whole thing! I had to pinch myself. My experience in Memphis was interesting, to say the least. From being able to mingle with physical education teachers from all over America and learn how they interpret the MYP, to staying in an icon of a hotel, The Peabody, and also attending an NBA game at the arena. I learned a lot during the conference and also through the interactions I had with others after the conference that will always stay with me. A learning memory that really does stick with me from this trip was playing American sports like American Football, but using all my knowledge of game sense to still be able to compete with the locals.

At the end of 2011, I had another opportunity to travel for professional development but for design technology. Please note that before coming to China I had never taught technology but the upside of teaching internationally was that my skillset grew. By 2011, I was the head of design technology and I needed some professional learning experience. So I was given the opportunity to fly to Hong Kong for an IB Asia Pacific Conference to learn more about design technology in the MYP. This again was an awesome experience as I got to spend three days with passionate design teachers and learn all I needed to learn about how to successfully implement and assess design technology. I learned more about what the design cycle is and how it can be implemented in all subjects and everyday life. I still use the design cycle to this day during certain units in physical education. It was something that could have only happened from going back to university and studying more but as a student, I was able to learn from others and that knowledge is still with me today.

As well as doing some other IB professional development during my first few years in China, I was also able to then participate in the East Asia Regional Council of Schools (EARCOS) Annual Teachers Conference in Manila, The Philippines. This was a great learning experience as this helped me to network with many other physical education teachers from around Asia. The conference itself was not just for the IB teachers but it was for any international teacher. I was able to get a good insight into certain physical education skills that other teachers were using at their schools and I also built up my knowledge around the use of technology in physical education classes. Once again this was at the expense of the school that I was working at and it was great to also travel with other teachers from that school as you can reflect with them at the end of each day and also find out what their learning experiences were like over the three days. From a professional side of things, I was able to learn from some of the best in the business. Andy Vasily and Ash Casey ran awesome workshops that really improved my skillset. Andy looked at how movement is more than just dance and gymnastics. It was fun to participate in and to this day I still use this knowledge with my classes, especially the 'Soul Train.' Ash's focus was on teaching games for understanding. Whilst I already knew much of this content, I still found it great to consolidate that what I was teaching and the way I was teaching had meaning in any type of curriculum. The most interesting memory I have of this conference was the fact that I caught swine flu whilst there as well as getting stranded at Manila airport for 12 hours due to a power outage.

In 2014, I made the shift to expand on my professional development skills. This involved applying to become a workshop leader with the IB. I was accepted into this post and participated in a five-day training course in Beijing. To this day, this training course is probably the best professional development I have done in my career. This professional development experience gave me the confidence to be able to stand up in front of a group of my peers and present my knowledge about certain areas that are in relation to the Primary Years Program. From gaining this qualification, I have been able to travel around Asia for the last six years and have had the pleasure to go to such countries as Cambodia, Vietnam, Singapore, Japan, China, and Australia. At each of these places, I was leading workshops to upskill teachers and I was also conducting school visits. These school visits involved evaluating the school to see if they meet the standards of the Primary Years Program. The school visits are a great form of professional development as you get to look deeper into how schools are operating and how they teach the Primary Years Program.

The Portable Profession

After spending eight years in Suzhou, China (a magnificent city where I met my beautiful wife and started a family), it was time to move on. We had been thinking about moving for a few years but we weren't ready, financially or mentally. A big advantage of living overseas is that you are able to save more money than you can in your home country due to the fact that you have expenses like schooling, medical, and housing that are paid by the school. After eight years we had saved more than enough to purchase a property back in Australia.

In 2018, my family and I moved to Japan to start teaching at an international school just outside of Tokyo. This was a big move for all of us as it was the first time my wife had lived away from her home comforts of family and friends and also for our young son, who only really knew China to be home. We knew that we were joining a well-established school with the hope that their professional development was of a high standard that could extend and expand my knowledge. Within the first six months of being at this new school, I was able to get a real sense of the importance of professional development here. The fact that I wouldn't have to travel too far to expand on my current knowledge as the staff that works there are all experienced and are so willing to share their knowledge, helps anyone to become a better teacher. During my first two years at this school, I was able to participate in what is known as the Collaboration for Growth (CfG). This is a professional development group of teachers from six different international schools throughout Asia that come together and create their own inquiries under the set topics that are of high importance for the schools that participate. This again is an amazing experience as I was able to sit down with very highly qualified teachers and pick their brains and find out answers to my inquiry.

Another one of the big professional learning experiences at my current school is that of what we call the Professional Growth Plan (PGP). This is where teachers are able to set a professional learning goal and then spend the year inquiring into it. At the end of that year, you are able to share your findings with the rest of the teaching community of that school. This is great because it isn't just you sitting down with a group of teachers who have similar interests, it is you going on your own professional learning journey and doing your own inquiry. This is so much more meaningful than the traditional model of professional learning communities (PLCs) that I have done in the past at other international schools and schools back home. Most importantly this form of professional development is about improving student learning and you do this by expanding your knowledge as a teacher and learning from other teachers with different experiences allows this to happen.

Professional development during COVID-19 has changed in so many ways. With people not being able to travel internationally and local schools not willing to have many people in one place, professional development has turned to the world of online. I was lucky enough that throughout 2020 I was able to participate in numerous professional development opportunities from the comfort and safety of my own home. In the first half of 2020, I participated in free webinars for school leadership, how to deal with the pandemic, and also how to teach inquiry physical education lessons online. Many of these courses happened over a few weeks or they are pre-recorded and then available for participants to watch in their own time.

With virtual professional development now becoming the norm for us all, it also provides a cheaper option for schools. These events happen after school hours and also on weekends. Another big difference is that there being breaks between sessions, allows teachers to spend a week or two implementing their new knowledge in their classrooms. They then can share their findings with the professional development group during the next sessions and improve on their teaching.

At my current school, we had the chance to work more closely with two highly regarded education gurus. In January 2021, we started working with Kath Murdoch on improving our inquiry knowledge and also on improving the curriculum for our elementary students so they can have more agency and ownership over their learning. In February of the same year, the whole school began working with Ron Ritchard on the cultures of thinking. Whilst many staff members at our school have attended one of Ron's workshops in the past, they felt that having it virtually and only involving our school, has really made it more personal and meaningful and they have been able to focus more on implementing some of the thinking routines and cultural forces in their own classrooms.

Advice for Others

Prior to leaving for your first international teaching position, see if you can participate in some professional development around the areas of conceptual learning, inquiry, and differentiation. Having more knowledge and experience in these areas is highly valued in the international community and will help you in the interview process.

For others who have just started international teaching then please do look at the opportunity to participate in professional development offered by your regions – EARCOS, ACAMIS, JCIS, NESA, ECIS, etc. All of these organizations offer a very high level of appropriate professional learning depending on the needs of the region so do look out for these opportunities. Some other great professional development opportunities are provided by the following groups – KSI (Knowledge Source Institute), ISS (International Schools Services), PTC / TTC (Principal Training Center / Teacher Training Center), and Chapters International to name a few.

My final bit of advice is for you to ask the following questions about a potential school's philosophy around professional development. Do they have a solid professional development program within the school? Do teachers have an allocated amount of money to use for professional development?

I hope this chapter has helped you gain a better understanding of what professional development looks like in the international teaching environment. I invite you to take the leap and join me on this adventure. You won't regret it!

Principals, Don't Wait for Retirement to Work Overseas

David Lovelin

My family's journey overseas began with this conversation with my wife, *"If we are looking at schools on the Oregon coast, then let's look at going somewhere else."* We didn't know anything at this stage about working in international schools but were at a point in our lives when we wanted to make a change, and with the challenges I continued to face, I wanted to feel like an educator again.

It was 2013, I was a high school principal at a large public school in my hometown of Gresham, Oregon. For the previous ten years, I had been in various leadership roles and working on my doctorate, all while starting a family. The life of a high school principal is all-encompassing and when my two-year-old daughter asked to visit me at my "home" (meaning my office), my wife and I knew we needed to make a change. We were not sure what the future would hold, but we were confident we needed to find some work-life balance for our family.

Coming back to the idea of working overseas, we decided we would do a deep dive to see what we could find out about working outside of the United States. During this search we found three firms; International Schools Services, Search Associates, and True Teaching. We contacted them, and within a week made the decision to leave Oregon. It was early November, when I notified my school district that I would be looking to move overseas in June. It is nerve-wracking to leave a great job in your hometown and throw caution to the wind, but my wife was the driving force, and together we were resolved to give our family a different way of life.

I applied to an incredible school in South Korea for a middle school principal position, and as all of the stars began to align, we knew this was

DOI: 10.4324/9781003133056-6

The Portable Profession

the right move for us. The interviews with the teams at the school were exciting, and the benefits package was going to allow us to travel and see the world. I accepted the job and now had to figure out how to break this news to our family.

We were sitting at Christmas dinner at my grandmother's home when we then shared this news of moving to Korea. The next few weeks were a blur as we broke the news and along the way the first questions were, "Why are you moving to Korea to teach English?" and, "Are you going to the North or South?" Looking back on these conversations, little was known about cultures outside of Oregon, and this proved to be difficult in the coming years.

Moving to South Korea posed some challenges, but we learned to be patient and navigate our new way of life. According to our kids there were many things that were 'weird' living in another country, but we learned living in another culture is not weird but different, and these differences created a new respect for our host culture. But it was not always easy. Every expat I know has had a moment when they ask themselves why they left their homes to move internationally.

For me, the first month of living in Korea was challenging. I was terribly sick, we struggled to navigate shopping for basic needs, and the heat and humidity were grueling. In that difficult moment, I knew I could not go back to Oregon. I was here (I signed a three-year contract), my family was here, and we just needed to find our way. Over the next few months I realized that I was really a toddler in an adult body as I learned to navigate transportation, communicate, read, and order food. I gained an important perspective and appreciation for Korea. Though difficult at times, we loved finding new shops, restaurants, temples, and hiking trails and our confidence grew in the weeks ahead as we carved out our own way of life.

When I first entered the campus of my new middle school, I was blown away by the facilities and support available to me. For the first time in my leadership career, I did not talk about budget cuts, salary freezes, managing the custodial staff, and fixing up classrooms. Instead, I was once again an educational leader being encouraged by an amazing and innovative director, Steve Cathers, to rethink the middle school program. He wanted the school to be a vibrant, project-based community, one where visible learning was paramount and finding creative teachers was critical.

Being given total freedom to design a program was awesome, but we were careful to make decisions with care and precision. I worked with a creative, student-centered team in this middle school and was fortunate to have on my staff a dedicated assistant principal. Both of us had a huge list of things we wanted to try but had never had the opportunity to do so. He was also new to the international world, having previously served as a K-6 principal in public schools on the east coast. Together, we spent many nights in the office ordering *chimaek* (spicy chicken and beer) or going to Korean BBQ for *samgyupsal* while planning the next stages of our middle school. After a couple of months and with our director's support, we began to shift the programs in a new direction, including integrated design and art programs, robotics, and engineering courses.

Over the course of three years, we hired the right people, gave them time to build and implement our changes, increased student agency, while incorporating a strong homeroom, and experiential education program.

Adding an experiential education program outside the walls of the school was a new concept for our community creating some new challenges. During the first roll out in a room of over 100 parents, the first question about the experiential education program was, "if we are going to miss three days of school when will the math lessons be made up?" Over many months, we had a dedicated team doing research and development on the benefit of adding an experiential education program and together we brought our parents along.

The experiential program focused on appreciating the beautiful environment and Korean culture while providing students the opportunities to push their boundaries and levels of independence. We organized trips for each grade-level in rural communities to learn about traditional Korean culture (music, salt farming, planting), food, while providing community service and developing meaningful community relationships. Many of our students had not spent a night away from their parents and had little exposure to the countryside and villages. One of my best experiences was our faculty singing campfire songs and building s'mores. I have many fond memories of sticky marshmallow hands and big chocolate smiles from a group of 100 middle school students!

During the transition of these programs, we learned how to adapt to the expectations and parameters within our host-country. As we developed a Maker Space, the idea of a 'garage' where students had access to build and create. As we provided access and training for our students, they loved it too but the power tools did freak out some of our parents and business staff.

The Portable Profession

We brought our parents into the school to experience these new classes, teaching them about the design cycle and completing design challenges. Over the course of a couple of years the parents became excited about the programming options and the school has continued to expand these experiences.

This shift was only possible because the Head of School wanted to create a different type of educational institution. Steve had a strong vision for bringing applied learning experiences to all grade levels, and he was committed to seeing this happen. I can only imagine the type of conversations he was having off to the side with parents and the business office but in the end he made it work. These changes did not cost a lot of money, but they did involve time and the ability to adapt and be flexible. The interesting thing about working in an international setting is that change can happen (in both directions) quickly and hiring the right people with a clear focus is critical.

Adjusting to Korea took about a year-and-a-half and we soon enjoyed the life that we were building. During the holidays we traveled to amazing off-the-grid vacations and met and made friends with people from all over the world. Each summer we would go back to Oregon and one year we had a BBQ and it happened at a time when we had a few colleagues from Korea. It was incredible to blend our life from Oregon with our new friends in Korea. Over the years many of our family and friends have traveled and visited us and it has been such a gift to share these experiences with loved ones.

After three years, an opportunity arose to move to Hong Kong. This was one of the most difficult decisions my wife and I had to make. The school community and education in South Korea had been incredible, and we knew we would miss the family dinners and watching one of our administrators dress up as Santa Claus for the kids at Christmas time. The care within this community was strong and it was going to be very difficult to leave, but we decided that we wanted to live in a place that was more culturally diverse and the prospect of moving to Hong Kong was a great opportunity.

Making the move to Hong Kong was exciting, but for our kids it was a real struggle. For them Korea was the first place they attended school and made friends. Over the course of many months there were lots of tears, Skype calls, and checking Facebook updates to help our girls adjust to our new life in Hong Kong. My wife and I also experienced a sense of loss that was unexpected. We made close friends in a very short amount of time in Korea and leaving them was hard.

Once we moved to Hong Kong, I was back in a high school principal role and in a school that was well resourced and wanted to make important changes to how students learn and experience education. Together with an awesome team of teachers and leaders, we worked hard to develop the school culture, student agency, and increase professional development for our faculty. We began incorporating the idea of a fishbowl based on a program developed in my previous school in South Korea, where we offered professional development throughout the day in micro sessions of 30 minutes. Creating a new space in the center of our campus provided a place where faculty could go to ideate, troubleshoot, and receive professional development with a team of educators that included an instructional technology coach, instructional coach, and curriculum coordinator. Together, they elicited feedback from our faculty and built sessions that teachers requested, wanted, and at times needed. With the support of the Interim Head of School, Dr. Ron Roukema, along with a school mission and vision that directly supported professional learning, we were able to develop this space over the course of a year.

We love living in Hong Kong as we enjoy the beaches, hiking, food, and culture. Our girls have made friends with kids of all ages, from different schools, and varied cultures. They enjoy playing on multiple sports teams and the ability to play in the ocean within a five-minute walk.

We are now in our seventh year living and working in Asia and continue to find new experiences that are fun, different, thought-provoking, and beautiful. Our kids are meeting friends from all over the world and the conversations and sharing of culture is astounding. As a family we have learned to be adaptable, resilient, understanding, and kind (both to ourselves and others) as we navigate our life overseas.

One of the reasons I love working and living overseas is our students' mindset and how their experiences of travel and charity work (service learning) impact the manner in which they view each other and the world around them. Our students are amazing, and we strive to support them. We have focused on providing formalized leadership training twice a year and creating an environment where they can lead, experiencing both success and failure in a safe atmosphere. We are now seeing the fruits of our labor, as each day I witness students looking for ways to make our high school community better. Students reach out to each other, and there is a real feeling of trust and care within our school walls. Like many schools in 2020, the community we helped create was tested this year, but the care of our faculty, students, and parents has never wavered and has made us even stronger.

Working and living overseas has impacted me and my family's lives tremendously. Over the past seven years, our family from Oregon have come to stay, we have visited 12 countries, and ridden motorcycles through Vietnam. Our kids played in soccer tournaments in Bangkok and Singapore, we experienced world heritage sites, and gained a deeper appreciation for culture and family. I don't know for sure where our road will lead in the future, but I am grateful to the mentors and educators I have had the pleasure to work alongside.

Advice for Others

Prior to moving overseas I had been an administrator for ten years in great schools in Oregon. During this time I worked alongside supportive mentors and many talented and dedicated educators, but it was tough. As we know working in administration is lonely and I found that working in Oregon I had no semblance of work life balance. There is never a good time to make the transition from home to somewhere far away. There will always be a sense of loss mingled with excitement and worry, but this opportunity will pass you by if you wait for the right time.

International school leaders also have an opportunity to increase knowledge within their educational system. In this role, I feel responsible for trialing ideas, mentoring others, and sharing our successes and challenges with other schools. I truly believe that many of our schools look and act like they are in the 1920s (bell schedules, students sitting at desks, specific days in the year) because we are not willing to take a step outside and try something new. The teachers we work with are brilliant, and together there is an opportunity to provide our kids with an education that is vibrant, caring, and with opportunities for autonomy and service above ourselves.

My wife and I plan to continue our time overseas, but the one thing we have learned by living internationally is that you never know what tomorrow will bring and where our paths will lead in the future.

SECTION

II

A Journey of Connectivism

George Siemens (2005) describes connectivism as "the integration of principles explored by chaos, network, and complexity and self-organization theories" (p. 5). Within the world of international schools, the degree of constant chaos within new environments is compounded by the amount of transition that happens within these organizations. International educators are in a constant state of transition with new colleagues, teams, and school leaders each and every year.

Connectivism could not be more aptly applied than it is within the world of international teaching. Connectivity is the one thing every international teacher has in common. With international educators, as soon as someone shares the location or name of their school, folks begin to drop names of educators they know who have either taught there in the past or are current teachers there now. The degrees of separation are far fewer than six. This connectedness allows teachers to get a feel of one another and who they know and align with. It might look like this, "You are at ABC School? Do you know ____? We worked together in ___." Or, "Did you overlap while ___ was teaching there?" You get the picture.

The second section of this book begins with Chapter 6. In this chapter, Elizabeth Onayemi discusses her "Whirlwind ESL Teaching Experience." The author takes us back to 2002 to Inner Mongolia where she shares stories of the complex English language learning industry of China. Chapter 7 is titled "Building Bridges in a Globally Diverse Setting," written by Sandra Chow. Sandra shares how she has built bridges and searched for identity both as a third culture kid (TCK) and as an educator. In Chapter 8, Jamie Bacigalup

DOI: 10.4324/9781003133056-7

focuses on the power of the memoir and helping students connect in "Community in the International Classroom: The Power of Storytelling." In the next chapter, Tsayli Lily Chang shares her search for identity and belonging within the world of international schools. The author shares the struggles of TCKs as they attempt to assimilate into new cultures in her chapter titled, "Belonging." Chapter 10 is titled "The Healing Power of an International Community." In this chapter, Elizabeth Cho intimately shares the connectivity and belonging international teachers experience while undergoing tragedy and hardship while overseas. Cho shares her journey of watching her husband face health challenges within a health system outside of her home country. The final chapter in this section focuses on transitions. In Chapter 11, Brenda Perkins discusses "Doing Change Well" as she details how teachers make the transition between schools and countries. The author explores ways to build credibility with new colleagues, finding one's tribe, and taking care of one's self during transition.

In this section, authors shared their journeys as they navigated the ever changing dynamics of new teams and colleagues within their schools. Through this chaos there remains a desire to make meaning fast and connect with others. The creation of an instructional environment is as important as the creation of a social environment for these educators. While overseas, expat educators often live within a fishbowl with their colleagues, living in housing units or on compounds. Together, these displaced educators share in the joy of a marriage, the birth of a child, and holiday traditions such as recreating a Thanksgiving meal in a country that does not sell turkey. This persistent change may also lead to quick friendships, and the sharing of intimate details of our lives and our relationships with family back home. This sense of connectivism can be incredibly strong when dealing with the death of a loved one back home or helping someone navigate the health system of a foreign country when they are faced with illness. The social environment of international school is definitely messy however international educators develop friendships and a new sense of family that last well beyond the borders of a map.

Reference

Siemens, G. (2005). Connectivism: A learning theory for the digital age. *Intelligent Decision Technologies Journal, 2*(1), 1–9. http://www.itdl. org/Journal/Jan_05/article01.htm

My Whirlwind ESL Teaching Experience in China

Elizabeth Onayemi

My first day in China in 2002 was very busy indeed. I checked into a huge hotel at a stadium, deposited my luggage, and then accompanied my host to purchase some basic necessities at a supermarket where I was astounded by the vast array of exotic-looking goods. We later purchased the train ticket that would ensure my safe passage to Baotou, Inner Mongolia. My host and I caused a bit of a stir at the train station as groups of what appeared to be laborers or farmers waiting for trains to their respective destinations turned to stare and point at us, often grinning, no doubt intrigued by our dark skin color. These people looked friendly enough and my host, who spoke some Mandarin, stopped to smile and greet some of them. Later that day, we dined not on Chinese food but rather at a McDonald's restaurant, my host's choice, and then headed up to a little bar where I listened to a Chinese rock band and had a taste of Tsingtao *pijiu*, a popular brand of Chinese beer. I later fell asleep with a smile on my face as the sights, smells, and colors of China swirled through my mind. The next day, I boarded a train to Baotou, seemingly the only foreigner and certainly the only black person on the train. The other travelers on the train were amiable enough, and I had a soothing uneventful journey in a sleeping cabin that had six passengers including myself.

I arrived in Baotou at the start of winter and was immediately immersed in Chinese culture. My employer, an English Second Language (ESL) agent who specialized in connecting foreign educators to Chinese public schools, met me at the train station with the friend who'd introduced me to his agency. They whisked me off to a Chinese restaurant where I was accorded a royal Chinese welcome and experienced my first taste of

DOI: 10.4324/9781003133056-8

exquisitely prepared Chinese delicacies. The other Chinese employees of the agency were waiting at the restaurant. We chatted and laughed and got to know each other. Fortunately, most of them spoke English.

Once the fanfare was over, I was briefed on my teaching assignment and cautioned about how extreme the winter was likely to be. "Life goes on," said my boss, the agency owner. "You will have to wake up every morning, go to sleep, go shopping, have fun, socialize, and have a normal life regardless of the weather." Well, forewarned is forearmed. I was given a grace period before starting my job. Within this time, I moved into a lovely apartment having outright rejected the dingy apartment they'd first tried to put me in. I loved my new home. It was on the third floor of the first block of an apartment complex in a tree-lined avenue on the outskirts of town on the way to the train station. Very suburban.

The ESL industry in China is complex. Some teachers are employed directly by private or public schools while others are employed by language training centers where they teach English to students after school hours and on weekends. However, sometimes teachers are employed by ESL staffing agents who hire them to teach at various institutions and maintain control over the teachers. My first employer in China was one such agent and as such, I was sent out to work at several institutions that the agency had English teaching contracts with. I taught at each of the institutions for a few hours each week and had a workload of about 30 hours per week. Being a very patient individual, or so I'm told, I proved very popular with the children.

I first taught at several schools affiliated with a large Baotou factory, many of which had auspicious sounding names such as The Number Four Middle School of the Baotou Iron and Steel Company. The classes were packed to the gills, sometimes with as many as 60 students. All the students that I taught had native Chinese teachers of English who taught them grammar and writing using English textbooks. My job was to engage them in conversational English and make the language appealing to them which I did enthusiastically through songs, blackboard games, and asking them to perform conversational skits. I was soon able to pick up additional teaching gigs at small private language training centers where middle-class parents took their children for private English lessons.

The private language training centers were fun to work at due to the smaller class sizes and the availability of resources including flashcards,

ESL Teaching in China

books such as *New Concept English*, and audio-visual equipment. I made many friends at these centers including fellow teachers, parents, and adult students. All good things come to an end and after two years in Baotou, where my last stint was at a prestigious high school, I found myself on a train heading to Hunan Province, the home province of Chairman Mao Zedong.

My Hunan teaching adventure started with tearful goodbyes to my Chinese friends in Baotou who I had come to treasure. I boarded a flight to Changsha, the capital of Hunan Province, a steaming hotpot of rustic Xiang Mandarin speakers known for their exotic cuisine which includes various dishes engulfed in red hot peppery sauces, stinky fermented tofu, and exotic meat stews amongst others.

I got my first job in Changsha fairly easily. I was appointed to teach ESL at a polytechnic in a district called Yuhuating. The job came with a lovely furnished apartment, free hot spicy meals at the school cafeteria; the usual ESL teacher benefits. The students were mature and friendly, the college atmosphere amiable, warm, and welcoming. The overseas liaison officer came across as being rather snotty, but it was easy to ignore her and focus on my lovely students. Also, there was a bigger problem that I had to deal with. In order to get a work permit, I had to exit the Chinese mainland and reenter the country. Hong Kong was my destination of choice for this purpose and the most affordable and logical option.

I arrived in Hong Kong aboard a train from Shenzhen. As I waited for a visa back to mainland China, I spent a memorable week shuttling between my tiny hostel cubicle in Kowloon Tang and the Main Island. I learned a lot about the island's cultural, social, and economic dynamics. I shopped and did a lot of sightseeing. I took a train ride up to the Peak where I visited Madame Tussauds and treated myself to a lovely star-lit dinner. I took a Hong Kong night tour bus ride and enjoyed the magnificent skyline of the Main Island. I ate noodles, dim sum, and fast food from KFC. I took the ferry ride every day and learned my way around sections of Kowloon Tang where I discovered affordable used clothing stores. I did all of this on my own, though an American friend helped by providing me with directions and general travel tips. I visited the outlying islands including Lantau and climbed numerous stairs up a mountainside to see the world's largest Buddha statue. Through conversations with my American friend, I learned about the benefits that proper international school jobs had over

35

ESL teaching jobs. My friend encouraged me to apply for those in the future since I already had a bachelor's degree in education.

Soon I had my visa and was ready to return to steamy Changsha. Things went pretty wrong upon my return to Changsha. Upon my arrival, the aforementioned overseas liaison officer informed me that a replacement was found during my one week's absence because the college administration assumed that I wouldn't return. This was despite the fact that I'd left all my personal belongings in my apartment on campus. A British teacher had been found, and she was staying in the hotel right next to the polytechnic waiting for me to vacate the apartment. We traded places and passed each other at the hotel door as I checked in because I had nowhere else to go.

So, there I was, jobless in a new Chinese city and miles away from home. I still had some money but was living in a hotel room wearing Chinese hotel paper slippers in the evening, watching Mandarin TV shows that I enjoyed but did not really understand, and drinking green tea to ward off the autumn cold. I subsisted mostly on bread, sausages, instant noodles, preserved eggs, and *guoji* (being orange juice). My mum urged me to return home to Kenya. I considered doing so but remembered the old adage, "winners never quit." A friend who was in the UK sent me some money to tide me over.

Resolve set in. I was determined to navigate the pitfalls of the competitive ESL job market. I did not have a laptop computer then, and my beloved desktop computer was still at home in Baotou waiting to be shipped to me by a Chinese friend along with the rest of my stuff. There was a cybercafé in a building across from the hotel. It was there that I spent my days and most of my evenings applying to jobs surrounded by a crowd of Xiang Hua speaking, cigarette smoking, betel nut chewing, lanky Chinese lads from the polytechnic. I hadn't left the neighborhood or the hotel at all because I was new to the city and figured I would be safer staying put, since I already knew the area. The lads at the café were nice enough, very courteous really. They peered at me through the smoky haze, smiled shyly, and went about their business as I churned out applications. The responses started rolling in.

One day, lady luck smiled on me unexpectedly. I got an email from an Irish lady who was an ESL teacher at a university. She also ran a teacher recruitment business on the side. The lady said she was recruiting for a university on the outskirts of Changsha. She had seen my resume and wanted

ESL Teaching in China

to meet me to discuss a teaching opportunity. I gave her the address of my hotel, and she picked me from there and took me out for lunch. We had an interesting conversation and she told me about her international student friends at the university where she taught.

Within a day of meeting the recruiter, the university sent a driver to take me to the campus for an interview. The head of the college suggested a trial lesson, which she observed along with a few teachers. The lesson went very well and I got the job, which came with furnished accommodation, return flights back home for the summer, and subsidized spicy food at the college cafeteria.

I began living and working on the suburban Chinese campus. I had a big house next to a scenic river surrounded by awe-inspiring tall trees, chirping birds, an ever-present chorus of croaking frogs, and an excellent group of expatriate teachers who soon became my good friends. There were tons of Chinese lecturers on campus but language constraints often prevented effective interactions with them. I made friends with numerous Chinese college students and have very fond memories of their many visits to my house where we cooked and ate sumptuous dinners, sang songs, had long and very interesting conversations, and watched movies. They were extremely kind to me and that helped to ward off homesickness.

A new chapter of my life had begun. One in which I met my husband and had my first-born child while teaching at that very same Chinese university. As we started our family, we started planning for the future, and I realized it was time to use my degree to find a better paying international school job, as previously advised by my friend in Hong Kong. I landed my first International Baccalaureate teaching job at an international school in Astana, Kazakhstan. Although I haven't returned to China since I left in August 2006, I will never forget the warm hospitality that I enjoyed when I lived there and I miss my Chinese friends who I long to see again one day.

Advice for Others

If you're a newbie to the industry, ensure that you've researched the international school job market well. Understand the difference between expensive K-12 international schools that cater mainly to expatriate children and upper-class locals, less costly K-12 international schools that cater mostly to locals, public and private national curriculum schools, cram schools, private language training centers, and so on. The options are wide and varied and have got different implications. They are also quite region-specific.

Another factor to consider is that students are important variables. Throughout my teaching journey, I have viewed my students as customers and this has served me well. Parents and organizations pay premium amounts to send their children to good schools and therefore have high expectations of these institutions. Likewise, such schools remunerate their teachers well expecting that the teachers will deliver high-quality lessons and create safe, happy, and enabling environments in which students thrive. It's essential for teachers to meet their side of the bargain.

Finally, it is also important to immerse yourself in the local culture and gain an understanding of your host country. While expatriate bubbles can be so enticing, take time to experience the local culture and understand the country in which one lives as an expatriate teacher. Interacting with students and teachers from local schools in the country in which I currently teach has brought me a lot of happiness. You cannot truly claim to have lived in a foreign country until you've made friends with some locals, tried out the local cuisine, visited local markets, traveled to some places, and learned to at least say hello in the local language.

Building Bridges in a Globally Diverse Setting

Sandra Chow

This is Sandra. She is a 竹升 *'djook sing'.*

I am a bridge builder. I didn't always think this about myself, yet I've come to the realization this is my identity, perhaps even my calling.

I was born and raised in the capital city of Ottawa, Canada where the dominant cultures were White and of European descent. I spoke Cantonese at home but was quickly immersed into French and English in school settings. Like many second-generation immigrants whose parents did not want them to lose their heritage, I also attended Saturday morning 'Chinese school' every weekend.

Growing up in a predominantly White environment, I frequently encountered statements like, "Wow! Why is your English so good?". Playful boys on the playground would pinch their eyes upwards and chant, "Ching! Chang! Chong!" I often felt like I stood out, rather than being part of the 'normal culture.' The boys' chants were confusing given I was fully immersed in North American TV culture and enjoyed Saturday morning cartoons, Sunday night Wonderful World of Disney, and weekday night sitcoms and dramas with my parents like everyone else. I was clearly the same as everyone else wasn't I?

While I longed to fit into the dominant White culture, I also lived in an alternative world that I enjoyed. This involved binging Hong Kong TV series on VHS tapes, singing the latest Hong Kong pop songs on karaoke, and hanging out with my mom's mahjong friends on weekends and their family (very much like the Joy Luck Club). Interestingly, my parents and their friends even had a term for living in these two opposing worlds, as I

DOI: 10.4324/9781003133056-9

was always referred to as a 竹升 'djook sing' – literally meaning 'bamboo ascending.' The implication of the name meant, I was like the inside of a bamboo pole, compartmentalized with shafts – I was neither here nor there. I was neither fully Canadian nor Chinese. I looked Chinese but my inside was Westernized.

Therefore, like many Third Culture Kids (TCKs),[1] my family background and community environment caused me great confusion, leading me to struggle with my identity. I took offense to my Chinese aunties calling me a *djook sing*, but at the same time I felt like they were not completely wrong. When new international students arrived at my school, I was often asked to translate or help out. This caused me embarrassment and anxiety because I felt like I was standing out, and being pulled away from the crowd. I was conflicted inside because I felt like my identity was my handicap.

Eventually my thinking matured and my sense of self-worth increased with this maturity. In fact, after being married for one year, my husband and I felt a calling to explore and understand our cultural heritage in greater depth. In 2007, we landed in Taiwan and taught at an international school in the capital, Taipei. Surprisingly, finding a job as a teacher was quite an easy process as my years of experience at a well-known public school district in Ontario had served me well. Additionally, my background showed adaptability and empathy to new cultures. My colleagues were a mixture of local Taiwanese staff as well as expatriates from around the world, however most called North America home. I became the go-to staff member for many of my non-Chinese colleagues to explain Chinese culture, translate, or navigate through cultural misunderstandings. I enjoyed being helpful, and almost felt like I had superpowers because I was confident in the culture and community of the Western school system, from which I was well trained, while also being very comfortable in the somewhat familiar Chinese context that we were surrounded by. Yet I was not quite a bridge builder at this point, I was rather more of a courier of information or a tour guide. My focus was much more on helping the expats and foreigners settle in, and adjust to their new context and environment. I needed a lot more perspective building and self-reflection to move forward in my thinking as a global citizen.

Nonetheless, living and teaching in Taiwan helped me to realize the blessings of my diverse Canadian upbringing and experiences. I felt like all my years of Chinese school learning did have a purpose, as I easily

Building Bridges

transitioned into a fully Chinese environment. The foods, smells, and sights, although a little bit different from the southern Chinese background that I came from, were similar enough that everything seemed familiar. I was able to read, write, and quickly pick up some Mandarin. Furthermore, both my husband and I gained a deeper understanding of our Chinese heritage, meeting one of our goals.

There were still many challenges moving to a new country and community with completely different systems. My elementary and karaoke level Chinese did not serve me as well when I needed to do banking, read contracts, and understand medical information. As a new expat living overseas for the first time, I needed to set up bank accounts, read rental contracts, and attend medical check-ups; all of which were in legalese Chinese. I found myself frustrated and struggling with the things that mattered most to me (i.e., finance, health, children's schooling). As much as I *looked* the Taiwanese part, I was still a foreigner in a foreign land. Although I had some superpowers, I still needed to rely on the hospitality and generosity of my local colleagues to support and guide me.

Moving overseas helped me to finally empathize and understand the challenges that my parents must have felt immigrating to a strange new country so many years ago. In 2011, with a now larger family, my husband and I decided to move back to Canada to have our children connect more with their grandparents. Back in my birth country, I realized my perspective and worldview had completely shifted. I was much more compassionate with the immigrant parents and families in the school where I taught. I made extra effort to help with banking and medical questions encountered by refugee and immigrant families. For newly arrived families, I prioritized time to go grocery shopping and to spend time with families to discuss their children's education options. It was clear to me, through my experience living overseas and teaching internationally, I had gained a great deal of perspective and learned to understand the needs of others who were either displaced or in a new cultural environment. I felt like I was previously blind to their challenges, but now I was much more sensitive and aware of the obstacles. I had learned empathy.

Although two of our kids were born while we were in Taiwan, they were little when we moved back to Canada in 2011. While growing up in Canada, we realized that our children were limited in their experiences and perspectives of the world. They had some diversity in their friendships,

41

and were able to experience some cultures through food, school, or vacation, but the experiences and exchanges were passive and shallow. As much as cultures and heritages are celebrated in Canada, the dominant culture is still Canadian. It became apparent for my husband and I, it was time for our family to move abroad once again. Except this time, our goals were not just about our own growth, but much more centered on our family, and how we could contribute as a family to the larger global community.

In 2018, our family landed at Keystone Academy in Beijing, China. Keystone is a not-for-profit private boarding school, with a clear mission to prepare students to be global citizens through the blending of Eastern, Western, and international education. There is an emphasis on bilingual immersion, and a priority on character education through the five shared Confucian values. Reading about the school and meeting the leaders, my husband and I knew that we had found our new home. We knew with our hearts that our family would grow and thrive in this new community.

Sure enough, since arriving at Keystone, my perspective and understanding of the world continues to stretch. Daily I learn from my local Chinese colleagues the merits and strengths of the Chinese way of teaching which surpasses the stereotypes of rote learning and memorization that myself and many Westerners associate with Eastern pedagogy. I'm starting to see opportunities for blending, collaborating, and innovating with the various methodologies, experiences, and traditions of teaching. Amazingly, our students express these possibilities the best as they experiment with the smashing of ideas and philosophies through their personal passion projects, like the blending of classical European music with traditional Chinese music, applying globalization psychology and the movement of people in their narrative writing, or experimenting with merging basketball and Wushu into a sport or art.

As a school, we take cultivating international mindedness and global competencies very seriously. We have looked into assessment tools like the Global Competence Aptitude Assessment (GCAA)® to measure dimensions of global competencies amongst staff and students; we collaborate with researchers from various academic institutions reviewing our curriculum and methods to enhance our students' understanding of the world; and we regularly reflect on our effectiveness as a school in collaborating together and utilizing the strengths of all our perspectives in our teaching.

As a family we have realized the unique blessings and gifts we have been given to be immersed in multiple cultures. My children, also bridge builders themselves, quickly adapted into their new school environment and made new expat and local friends. It amazes me to see how quickly my children can switch easily between Chinese and English depending on who they are talking to. Our school is a beautiful mosaic of educators from different countries and our children have the privilege of learning and living in community with them on a daily basis. My five year old regularly plays on the playground with his little friends, while various *Nai Nai's* or *Ye Ye's* (Grandmothers or Grandpas) supervise nearby. My eldest has developed a passion for both badminton and basketball through the regular evening gym nights hosted by the physical education teachers or coaches. My colleagues have become our global family, and together we speak into our children's lives while together on a mission to serve the larger school village. It is an experience that is truly unique to being a part of an international school community.

I'm still a work-in-progress, but I'm neither a *djook sing*, nor just a tour guide anymore. Taking active steps to build understanding and collaborative opportunities between our colleagues with various backgrounds is a priority for me, and sharing this learning has also become my passion. I believe that connecting with others who can spur you on in a journey of self-reflection, global explorations, and cultural perspectives is critical. If we could all build bridges and actively strive to blend our thinking and understanding from different perspectives, think of all the new possibilities and innovations that could result!

Advice for Others

I hope I have piqued your interest in the possibilities and excitement of teaching internationally. There is truly a tangible day-to-day experience of living as a global citizen when teaching abroad. The experience comes with the struggle of identity, challenges of living in a completely new environment and culture, and frustration of not always understanding. However, the rewards of such experiences are rich and plentiful.

Furthermore, preparing to be global citizens can happen anywhere and everywhere. While it is much more experiential when living abroad, we can all learn to be a little bit more open-minded when talking to others from different cultures. Develop curiosity in getting to know people, their traditions and their perspectives, and encourage your own children to be curious as well to broaden their thinking. Be adventurous in experiencing the variety of cultures that exist wherever you are. This could be as simple as trying various ethnic foods, visiting a place of worship, or inviting people into your home and vice versa. Be mindful to foster diverse friendships, especially for your children, through classroom interactions, extra-curricular activities, and playdates.

Identify your own biases about people by taking assessments (e.g., Intercultural Development Inventory, GCAA) and being more reflective. Challenge these biases by diving deeper into these ideas, experimenting with new frameworks, and applying them into your actions and practice.

Most importantly, embrace differences and build bridges.

Note

1   https://www.nytimes.com/2020/09/11/t-magazine/luca-guadagnino-third-culture-kids.html

Community in the International Classroom
The Power of Storytelling
Jamie Bacigalupo

In 2012, I found myself on a school bus in Ecuador. As a newly minted international school teacher, educating high school students at Colegio American de Quito, I was sitting next to a colleague from New Zealand named Jeanette. She was telling me about the international adventures that she and her Iranian husband had been on thus far, and their plan to continue teaching abroad for years to come.

As I listened to Jeanette tell me of the tapestry of her life, my Midwestern heart was bleeding to be home. *What am I really doing here?* I wondered. *Why would anyone choose to live and teach abroad long-term? Will I ever feel at home in this strange place?*

Over the course of three years in Quito, the woman that had been sitting on the bus with Jeanette, drowning in homesickness, became a woman who fell in love with her host city, fell in love with her life abroad, and fell in love with the feeling of home and the sense of community that flourished in this new place.

In choosing a life as an international educator, I reflect time and again on how we develop community inside of our classrooms. The choice to move abroad had proved nearly excruciating that first year, and it had been *my* choice. The students in front of me each day are there because of their parents' decisions, their parents' jobs, their parents' journeys.

DOI: 10.4324/9781003133056-10

A Journey of Connectivism

Each August when we begin school, I gaze out at my students, wondering about the individual origin stories that brought us all to this classroom in China. Looking at each individual student, I wonder, are they excited to be here? Worried? Anxious? Do they feel a sense of belonging here in China? Is it a home away from home, or simply a house away from home?

When I first began teaching at Shekou International School (SIS), I asked my tenth-grade students to write memoirs as part of our first unit of the school year. The writings were fine. Some were good. But there was also something missing in the process and the product. Something lost and not yet found.

In my third year of teaching at SIS, in collaboration with three colleagues, I developed an oral storytelling component to the unit, and we named it SIS Stories. Rather than writing narratives with the teacher as the primary reader, I wanted my students to have an audience more authentic and diverse. In expanding the unit to include oral storytelling, we found what had been lost before: An appreciation for our varied experiences and an appreciation for the universal emotions expressed in each story.

Perhaps more than any other context, international classrooms hold a unique uncertainty for students (and teachers). Some students have been planted in Chinese soil for a number of years, others are wondering if they will ever grow roots here. Many students walk the school halls questioning, *When will I leave or be left behind?* This uncertainty can make it difficult for students to be willing to connect deeply and to be vulnerable. Through the memoir and storytelling unit, I wanted to use the power of story to help students see that in leaning into vulnerability they could form meaningful connections to their peers and weave a tapestry of community.

Each year, I ask students to write around a common, open-ended theme which has included: First Sight, Enter/Return, and Origins. I want my students to take their interpretations of these themes in unexpected and unique directions, and to eventually see that there are common threads that connect their lives to their classmates.

As I was introducing the unit this year, already anticipating with visceral excitement the big oral storytelling event, I watched my tenth graders look around the room with reservation. In their looks, I read uncertainty and insecurity, and *Is this lady crazy? Does she think we are going to stand in front of each other without a Keynote and just tell a story for ten minutes?*

In my experience as a teacher at SIS, I have found most international students to be compliant with the rules and expectations. For this reason, I knew the students would indeed get up and do what I asked of them.

But, as a teacher of the heart, I was not seeking compliance. I wanted true buy-in. I wanted enthusiasm from them like the excitement I was feeling.

I had to work for their heartfelt engagement, and that is fair. Asking students to step into vulnerable spaces is asking them to access deep courage. I began by modeling it myself.

After reading excerpts from memoirs like Trevor Noah's *Born a Crime* and Roxane Gay's *Hunger*, we began to ideate on our own origin stories. At the beginning of class one day, I pulled up my list of ideas, showing it to my students:

- Tutoring Danny: The origin of seeing myself as a teacher
- Obsession with Food Network: The origin of my chef self
- Move to Quito, Ecuador: The origin of an international career
- April 2019: The origin of a cat-mom-life to two cats
- Panic attack the summer going into sixth grade: The origin of my intimate relationship with anxiety

As a few more days of writing wore on, we came to a place in the unit where I wanted the students to start sharing their drafts with one another. I first put my own draft in front of them. Before we read my writing, and before they offered me feedback, we discussed ways to offer constructive feedback.

Once students were engaged in peer conferences, I walked around the room. I heard William, deeply rooted after five years at SIS, reveal, "I've never had a friend up until 5th grade." I listened as Demi, a newly planted student, shared, "In books, love was described as something fiery and passionate, like something burning strongly inside of you…"

Before we closed class for the day, I caught Shanshan bravely sinking her first roots into SIS soil, opening up to her newfound friend. Her voice was soft and a bit uncertain as she read from her computer:

> It was a quiet evening filled with tension. I looked at the building in front of me, where my new journey would begin. It looked fine from the outside, but still, I sighed—It was my first time transferring to a new school, and I wasn't the type of person that's good at making new friends.

After my students left my classroom, I looked out at the diamonds the sun was creating on the South China Sea. I reflected on what my kids were learning as they began to reveal parts of their international lives. As I had listened to the conversations, what impacted me the most was the variety of paths that led to this same destination; a classroom in Shenzhen. We were beginning to weave our individual tapestries into a collective class-room tapestry.

We continued to share and write and revise and be more courageous in the details we included in our stories as the weeks passed.

When the students walked into class on the day of SIS Stories, they passed a standing banner emblazoned with *SIS Stories* and photos from the previous years. The banner was symbolic of the rite of passage this tenth-grade oral storytelling event has become.

The room hummed with nerves and anticipation and excitement. We would be recording the students' stories to make a podcast; this added to both their enthusiasm and their anxiety.

Yelim, a Korean national in her second year at SIS, was the first to tell her story.

> I don't remember that many details from the time me, my mom, and my sister went on a trip to Australia. I was 9 at the time and all I remember are the smallest and most random details. I remember seeing the opera house under a bright summer sky. I remember eating a beautiful chocolate-coated ice-cream cone in front of some church. I remember that people in Australia really loved to eat steak.
>
> I also remember that an old man I met on a bus called me fat.

In the hushed silence, our bodies collectively leaned towards Yelim, into her vulnerability, and into her story. She began to relax, sharing with us the way she has come to regard her body in a more positive light now than she did a decade ago.

One student after another stood to share the pieces of their lives that have woven them into the beings they are today. Some students had shaky voices, some students let tears fall from their faces in front of the class, and some students stopped to start over and finish their story in triumph.

The last student to tell her story was Seyun. She had arrived at SIS two years prior from a Korean public school.

"I was on the number 6 school bus. It was chaos happening right in front of my eyes," she started.

The Power of Storytelling

As I listened, I was back on that bus in Quito, relating the chaos I had felt then to the chaos that Seyun was describing now.

"Every moment that I was capturing since I stepped inside the school was different from what I used to see in Korean middle school. Different in a good way," explained Seyun.

What a marvel this student is, what beauty these students are, who can step into new international settings and find peace and comfort so quickly, I thought to myself.

> To be honest, I did miss my old school and old friends and I was also frightened of changes before I arrived at the campus. But when I was standing in the moment in SIS with my advisory members, the changes coming to me didn't look so bad,

Seyun continued.

I thought back to those first days and months of teaching abroad again, remembering the rawness, the hardness, and the moments of wonder that I had experienced, the moments where I finally began to feel that the changes my life had undergone didn't look so bad.

As Seyun finished her story, tears pricked my eyes when she said, "One of the questions I asked myself while riding the bus that morning was 'will I regret deciding to move to SIS?' And my answer was, 'No, I will not.'"

Me either, Seyun, me either, I thought to myself.

What an incredible big-small world I have come to see in my time as an international school teacher. A world in which a teacher and her student, in different times and different places, are both sitting on a bus, contemplating what twists and turns their lives have taken. A world in which the teacher and student end up in the same space, woven into a community.

Advice for Others

International teachers supporting and nurturing their students face the challenge of fostering community. When students arrive in our classrooms, they are often wondering how much effort they should put into new relationships, how much vulnerability they should show, and if they or their new friends are simply going to move in the next month or the next year. My most profoundly simple advice to the reader is to use personal storytelling to support the community in your classroom. We may wonder how much of ourselves to commit to new relationships with transient people, but the fact is, the most beautiful parts of our humanity are in need of those true connections.

Belonging

Tsayli Lily Chang

On a blustery Friday morning, my partner and I trudged through knee-deep snow to get to our very first international school job fair. This was the ISS-Boston job fair held every February. It was at this job fair that we kicked off our career as international educators by landing jobs at the Seoul International School. Friends and families often ask us, "Why do you want to leave the US?" or "Why do you want to pack up your whole life, leave your friends and families, and move to a foreign land?" I suppose, in order to answer these questions, we would have to go back in time, back to when my family immigrated to New Jersey in the United States in 1998 when I was nine. For me, it was this move that made a profound impact on my worldview and my sense of belonging.

When my family immigrated to New Jersey, it transformed me into what is called a third culture kid (TCK). A TCK is a person who was raised in a culture other than their parents' or the culture of their country of nationality, and/or lives in a different environment during a significant part of their developmental year. Becoming a TCK meant that I moved between and within cultures. I learned to adapt to the culture in New Jersey by listening to pop music, talking about boys, watching current TV shows, and even getting a tattoo like everyone else in high school. I did everything that I was supposed to do, in order to fit in with a predominantly Caucasian, homogenous population where everyone knew each other since kindergarten. Wanting to dress like everyone else, I had many heated arguments with my mom over what was 'appropriate' and what was not. I pretended to know all the pop culture references that predated my existence in the US by laughing along. I learned to speak English with as little accent as

DOI: 10.4324/9781003133056-11

possible and was often confronted with the remark "Wow, you speak such fluent English." I joked along with others when they made racist remarks like, "Did you jump off a boat?" or "Which rice field did you work on?" all the while asking myself, "I don't belong here, do I?" Because if I did belong here, I would not be made fun of in such a way that made me feel lesser than.

While I did as much as I could to assimilate with the New Jersey culture, I was able to hold on to my Chinese heritage. Looking back, I am forever grateful to my parents who forced me to speak Chinese with them at home. The fact that they watched Chinese soap operas and entertainment shows every night provided me with the opportunity to watch along with them. My older brother, who kept listening to Chinese music, was yet another way that I was able to stay up to date with the Chinese culture. He also often took me along with his Chinese friends to karaoke which helped me stay connected with other Chinese people. Through my family, I was able to stay plugged in with my native language and culture. So, as I finished off my high school career and began to embark on my journey at Rutgers University, I learned to straddle both cultures. However, like many TCKs, there would be that nagging feeling of belonging to both cultures yet belonging to neither culture. I realized that having a sense of belonging is not as simple as dressing and talking like everyone else around me.

Once I got to college, I tried to *find* my identity and was eager to fulfill that sense of belonging. My first attempt to find that identity was broadening my social group by building relationships with people from diverse backgrounds. I made friends with and dated people from a wide range of ethnicities but never with another Chinese or Chinese American. The irony is that I felt threatened whenever I was around another Chinese person. This, I came to find out many years later, is known as a social identity threat. It is something that I did not overcome until very recently, which could well be another book chapter on its own!

Through college, I thought that maybe I could find an ethnic group that I connected with more than Caucasians. However, doing what all university students did, I studied, I partied, and I got distracted by college life. The need to feel that I belonged fell to the wayside and was no longer a priority. Whenever the need did pop up, I would tell myself, "Aren't all college students going through the same thing? Aren't we all trying to figure out what major to choose? What life path to take? I am no different than

Belonging

any other college student." This feeling, I told myself, was normal. Then, I met someone, who would end up being my husband. We clicked, we bonded, and we fell in love. We finished university and joined the real world. We fell into a comfortable pattern of adulting. We found 9-to-5 jobs. We bought new cars. Being in a stable relationship with a stable life, I was under the illusion that I had found where I belonged. Then one fateful event brought my need to belong right back up to the top of my list: My brother's wedding in Taipei.

This was my first time back to Taipei since I left when I was nine. At the time, that was a 14-year gap. I embraced Taipei in a way that I couldn't imagine. For the first few days, I enjoyed all the delicious food, the flurries of visiting family members, and not being the only Asian girl wherever I went. There was a sense of comfort that I didn't feel in my life back in the US. I was shocked at the multitude of emotions that I was feeling and the word 'belonging' came back to me once again. I realized how I had confused the comfortable pattern of adulting as a sense of belonging. As the days went by, my life in the U.S. became less and less appealing. I returned to the U.S. with a sense of urgency. I was back on the mission to find that missing sense of belonging.

Fast forward two months. I convinced my partner to pack up our belongings, quit our jobs, and embark on overseas living. We moved to Taipei because I wanted to revisit the feeling that I had when I previously visited during my brother's wedding. It was freeing to not have to try so hard to fit in. It was refreshing to just blend in with all the other Chinese people and not feel odd to stand out in a crowd for being the only Asian person. But, alas, the honeymoon period (no pun intended) ended when family members began to label me as the "foreigner" or "American." Whenever I spoke Chinese, people would give me a look and ask "did you grow up somewhere else? You don't sound like a local Chinese." My heart would sink. Once again, I didn't truly belong here either. I quickly realized that belonging is also not surrounding myself with people who looked like me. As I began to question the move to Taipei and regret leaving my life in New Jersey, I became obsessed with finding the answer.

I started to talk more openly about what I was going through and the topic of belonging was my favorite conversation starter with friends and family. Here's the funny thing. The more I talked about this, the more I found out that others had gone through or were going through a similar search

53

themselves. This ability to talk openly about belonging became the turning point. I started to meet people who could relate to how I struggle with my sense of belonging. One of the biggest reasons that propelled many of them to leave their home country was this same search for belonging. Alas, I had found a group of people like me who were going through the same journey.

In the four years that we lived in Taipei, I ended up meeting a lot of expats who professed a similar search for a sense of belonging. It wasn't always ethnically related either. For some people, it was due to sexual orientation. For others, it was a rejection of the traditional lifestyle of a 9–5 job with 2.5 kids and a white picket fence house. Yet, for others, it was simply wanting to find people like themselves who appreciated living a nomadic life. Whatever the reasons might have been, it felt so good to finally meet fellow brave souls who were in search of their own sense of belonging.

Slowly, the answer to this burning question dawned on me: A sense of belonging is not achieved by dressing oneself like others, talking like others, looking like others, or worse, drowning oneself in the mundane routines of life. A sense of belonging is to be able to find a group of people who accept me for who I am and who I can connect with on an emotional level. The expats were a group of people that I was able to connect with because we've all shared this journey of searching. We've all struggled to fit into our own home country somehow. We've all had a hard time connecting with people who wanted us to change so that we can conform. Having the bravery of tearing oneself out of the comfort of one's own country and to travel to a new unknown, is also an important life experience that served as the glue that bonds us all under the label 'expats.'

Living and working in Taipei, my partner and I came in contact with fellow international educators. As soon as we found out that international educators are people who traveled and taught in international schools around the world, we thought, "This was it!" The idea of meeting other expats and living among expat communities around the world sounded like heaven.

And so, this brings us back to the beginning of the story, back to that ISS-Boston job fair where we landed our first international school job. Why did we think it was a good idea to pack up our lives, leave our friends and families, and move to a foreign land? It was so that we could join a group of people, who like me, found a sense of belonging in the expat community. We all traveled far away from home so that we could feel like we belong.

Belonging

Advice for Others

If you are a TCK like me, do not hesitate to speak out and/or seek support from others. The challenges and struggles of an identity crisis are real and the more support you have the better you are equipped to handle them. Search for 'third culture kids resources' and you will get a plethora of results, here are just a few to get you started.

- Families in Global Transition
- Interaction International: Daraja
- TCKid NOW

As I begin my seventeenth year as an expat, I continue to meet people who feel more at home in a foreign land than in their home country. I am still amazed by how open and accepting fellow expats are with each other. How people adopt each other as *friendmilies* (friends that become your overseas family). This, I believe, is one of the best reasons to join and be a part of an international school community. If you've ever felt the same way that I've felt, needing to find a sense of belonging, give international teaching a try. Once you are ready to take that step into the world of being an international educator, be sure to sign up with reliable firms/agents to ensure that you secure a job with reputable schools.

The Healing Power of an International Community

Elizabeth Heejin Cho

I loved hanging out with my grandmother as a kid. As the youngest of four, I often kept to myself and was too shy to play with other kids. Grandma always encouraged me to go make friends outside, though she graciously and happily kept me company. She loved to watch Korean dramas, so naturally, I'd sit next to her and watch, too.

The best '80s K-drama plot consisted of, in my childhood mind, three possible conflicts intertwined in a series of coincidences: The rich, evil person vs. the poor, good person; the wicked mother-in-law who lays down the choose-me-or-her ultimatum to her son; and lovers who finally get together but will inevitably be torn apart as one coughs up blood surreptitiously into a handkerchief and has a limited number of days to live. I remember role-playing the sad scenes and crying over the tragedy of the pending farewell that must come as one lover dies, coughing into squares of toilet paper pre-marked with my mom's red lipstick for 'blood.' Grandma would see this and reassure me, "You just wait. The storyline will get better, I promise."

Maybe I always had a flair for the dramatic, but even so, to experience the gut-wrenching moment of devastating truth, in reality, is not something anyone is ever prepared for, no matter how many times you may have unwittingly imagined it as a kid.

My gut punch came on July 3, 2018, in the parking garage of a casino in Indio, California, where we sat, numb, confused, left with so many uncertainties. The nurse practitioner on the speaker of my husband's cell phone said, "It's odd that this wasn't noticed until this late stage." And there we were, just stuck on the words, "late stage."

DOI: 10.4324/9781003133056-12

Healing Power of International Community

On the eve of Independence Day in the U.S. at 4:00 PM, especially out in the middle of a desert, there is no one you can call to ask questions. To run more tests. To tell you that we've come so far in our medical advancement that we have a treatment for late-stage melanoma, which otherwise might as well have been a death sentence ten, even five years ago. And thus, Mark and I officially faced our worst 4th of July as we held each other in tears of epic proportions, nonstop streams of confusion simply gushing out of us both, the confusion that held us with doubt and fear of the unknown, afraid that there may be an untimely goodbye to come without daring to say it aloud. A cruel joke, just when we had decided it was time to grow our family.

We found Mark's cancer because we had moved to Korea for our next international school placement, a country of plastic surgery and casual procedures performed to remove any unflattering blemishes or scars. The dermatologist had simply asked, on a routine check-up, as all others had asked him in the past, "How long have you had this keloid on your scalp? Does it bother you?" And with the response, "Well, it never has for years but recently I've bumped it a few times and it's bled here and there," the doctor made a suggestion.

"Do you wanna remove it? It's a pretty big eyesore. And it's an easy procedure."

"Sure," Mark replied. Why not, we thought.

As the doctor removed the raised bump and followed up to check on the remaining scar, he told Mark, "I don't like how it's growing back, and the wound does not seem to be healing. I'm going to write you a referral for a biopsy. I recommend that you get this checked out." This, a week before we left to go back home to the U.S. for summer break, and without thinking much of it, we flew home.

Fast forward to that phone call in Indio.

Fast forward again to July 21, 2018.

After the surgery to do a wide, local excision on Mark's head, we were in high spirits. We were ready to return home to Korea for my first year at the Korea International School, Mark's second. We were sure there would be no metastases found in his lymph nodes that were removed from his neck during his surgery. Much to our dismay, when we got the call that melanoma was found in his lymph nodes, we sat numb once again. This phone call was a confirmation that Mark was indeed in stage 3b with desmoplastic melanoma.

Late stage, she had said.

Stunned, we went through our options. Not returning to work was a possibility, but we decided that we were not going to let cancer stop us from living, to assume the worst before fighting, to sit and weep the way we had done the first two weeks of the news. So, we were going to go back to our life in Korea. Pragmatically speaking, stopping work meant no health insurance, and we knew having that was imperative, with what we later found out would cost $12,000.00 USD a month. We made the decision together that while Mark stayed in the U.S. longer to map out the next steps, I should return first as there was nothing else I could do. I couldn't make cancer go away, and I had no magic potion to help Mark's wounds heal.

Being back in Korea without Mark was surreal. A week felt like one long, never-ending day. While I don't remember the details of work or my other comings and goings, I will never forget the community that embraced me. Dinners. Walks. Wine dates. Hands to help arrange the new apartment that we had moved into just before we had left for the summer, with boxes and furniture everywhere. When Mark eventually returned with plans to continue immunotherapy in Korea, my head of school instituted a "Crazy Hat Day" to welcome Mark on his first day back. What an image it was to see all the hats that were worn to help Mark blend in! I wish I would've taken photos, but I was so overwhelmed with love that I only have mental snapshots in my memory.

As the treatments began, KIS teachers donated their sick days to us so that we could go to Mark's appointments together once a month. I was able to be with him from start to finish, hand in hand on the train ride as well as in the hospital bed. I could hold him when his excruciating headaches began in the afternoon and continued into the night, a side effect of the medication. This gracious gift without a second thought allowed us the balance we needed to stay focused in every aspect of what we were doing, both professionally and personally, giving our all in everything we did.

There is something beautiful about international school communities. The like-mindedness of world travelers who can empathize with the hardship of leaving biological family members behind in our home countries makes for beautiful satellite home communities. KIS was no exception.

Beyond our immediate school community, we reached out to our friends all around the world, thanks to our international teaching life, when we found out about Mark's cancer. I made our story public on social media.

Healing Power of International Community

Though as private as I was, we had experienced the power of connectivism professionally and felt we could use that power now, personally, in our lives. Our experience made us believe that as we geared up to bat the unexpected curveball life hurled at us, we needed every encouragement and perspective of the half-full glass, to continue learning through this process. It made perfect sense to harness all the positive energy we could garner. So we told our story and opened up our journey for others to join, no matter how near or far.

The result of our sharing was an astounding overflow of love and support from around the world. Our friends visited us from New Zealand, Guatemala, Thailand, and China. We had packages arrive with notes of encouragement and love, items of personal connection, and items to make us laugh in the midst of these hard months. While Cancer raged her might against us, Mark and I were reminded to be grateful for the international lives we had lived that allowed us this outpouring of love... from *everywhere.*

Although grief seemed to be snapping at our heels every step of the way, encouragement clung to us closer through our international community, teaching us a whole new meaning of *family.* A family became to us much more than "a group of one or more parents and their children living together as a unit" as defined by the Oxford dictionary. To us, *family* meant a group of people living together as a unit, period, wherever they are, by looking out for each other, lifting each other up, and building genuine friendships that transcend time and space so that we feel rich and full through any challenge. Our lives as international educators taught us that.

Our China family sent us hats galore for Mark to wear with personalized messages that filled our apartment with tears and laughter. Hats of rabbit ears, poop emoji, rasta dreads, cowboy – you name it, we got it. Our Korean family joked and laughed with us over how Mark's perfectly bald circular head-scar from the wide excision would make for a good beer coaster. They came over to bring us Christmas cheer with all the decorations when we had no energy left after an exhausting semester, with still seven more months of treatment to go. Our global family flew in to see us and wrote to us every month that we went in for Mark's treatment. Without the international teaching experience abroad, we would've never had this.

In sharing our story openly, something else incredibly unexpected happened. We found out a friend within our professional network had also the exact same diagnosis as Mark at just about the exact same time.

A real-life coincidence – what were the chances? She had been struggling to cope, to accept, but by seeing our journey online, she began to process her own and found the courage to share, too. We loved getting to see her in Bangkok, and the two of them could exchange stories of their respective reactions to Opdivo[1] during immunotherapy. My heart smiled as I saw my two friends finding a small bit of emotional reprieve over dinner as Empathy held them close.

The rich evil Cancer tried to suck us financially dry, but she didn't have a chance as our international insurance paid us back each month's medical expenses. As for my farthest-from-evil mother-in-law, she was simply elated that her forever-vowed-to-be-a-bachelor son chose his best friend to marry, happy that love gave him the choice of life over despair when the news of his cancer hit. My dramatic reality as it turns out didn't end up with an untimely farewell, albeit some blood splatters along the way.

Fast forward to November 2020.

Pause.

Give cuddles and kisses to Finlay, our five-month old son.

See that the glass is still half-full, despite the global pandemic.

This has been the best storyline yet, and I still hear and trust the promise that it'll only get better. If my grandmother could see me now, she would be so proud that I stepped outside of my comfort zone to make new friends. In fact, I think she'd be pretty shocked at how far I made it past our front door. I know that Mark and my journey isn't over as we continue the rest of our lives with scans, blood work, and tests, but we also know that our family that extends to all corners of the world will always be there for us to pull us through anything.

Advice for Others

Sometimes people are hesitant to take the leap to teach abroad because they would be leaving everything they know behind, everyone they love. However, I cannot imagine having had to deal with my husband's illness anywhere else, because (1) being able to teach abroad has extended our family of friends far and wide and therefore our support system that much deeper; (2) health insurance and health care in Korea were beyond what we would have gotten in the U.S.; and (3) we were able to travel to countries like Malaysia, Hong Kong, Thailand, Vietnam, and Singapore during his treatment year to replenish our spirits while continuing to grow as educators at various conferences. We of course still got to go home during the longer holidays (and still do) to connect with family and friends there, too.

My advice is to take the leap if you're on the fence. Every stage you experience, the good and the bad, will be a time worth remembering.

Note

1   Medication used to treat a number of types of cancer.

Doing Change Well
Brenda Perkins

Many teachers spend an average of five to ten years at a single international school before moving on to a new school, new country, and new adventure. Thus, if you are a beginning international school teacher that intends on making a life overseas, you can expect to move at least three to five times or more, in your career. How we choose to respond to the challenges of these changes, even if the changes are of our own choosing, can be the difference between you and your family thriving in a new country or struggling on a daily basis. It's important then to consider how you might want to 'do change well.'

I have been an international teacher for over 25 years, working in schools in Egypt, Thailand, and now Taiwan. I have had many roles throughout my career – science teacher, department chair, team leader, health and well-being educator, and counselor. However, an aspect of my career is rather unusual in international schools: I spent 23 years at a single international school and then moved to a new school this year. It's been a very challenging journey that has made me consider the concept of change a lot this year. Leaving my school after so many years has been very challenging and upon reflecting on my experience, I want to share three lessons I've learned about 'doing change well' in a new school: Build credibility; Find your people; and Take care of yourself.

Lesson 1: Build Credibility

Being new at a school is hard. I expected it to be. I'm not so sure that mentally knowing it was going to be hard quite prepared me for it being so

DOI: 10.4324/9781003133056-13

Doing Change Well

hard! Moving to a new job internationally means not only are you changing your workplace, but you are changing your home, your community, and your country. Professionally, one of the most challenging aspects has been the loss of my credibility. After having worked at the same school very successfully for so long, I enjoyed a great deal of credibility. I had a lot of 'money in the bank' as it were, and I had already earned the trust of my colleagues and families. My reputation was a privilege that was hidden to me until I moved. All I could see was the beautiful forest I had lived in, and I had forgotten about all the trees I planted. When you move to a new school, you have zero trees planted. Sure, your resume and references got you the job, but few people in your new school will ever read either of those. You have to start rebuilding your credibility from the first email you send on your new account and the first day you step foot in your new school.

I really failed to understand how significant this would be when I moved. One fact became apparent; my *credibility* was very closely linked to my *identity* in my previous school and community. Who was I in my new school? In my previous school, I felt like I was a passionate teacher, a committed leader, a trusted colleague, a valued member of the community. All of that seemed to vanish overnight. The anchor of my identity was cut and I felt adrift in my new school and new role. Many people gave me advice for this first year – and basically, it was "talk a little and listen a lot." But I wasn't hired to just shut up and listen! I was hired to do all the things I used to do at my old school! I wanted to prove to my administrators and colleagues I was worth my salt!

And then I remembered something important. My salt isn't worth anything if I don't have credibility. And how do you gain credibility? Listen. Seek to understand where you are. Be curious about everything. Wonder…out loud…a little. Be good at your job and continuously seek to be excellent. Ask questions that help your new colleagues see things from a beginner's perspective. Be collaborative. Stand up for changes you believe in but be willing to do the hard work to make it happen. Listen some more. Listening isn't just about paying attention to what is being said at the moment but also listening to the history of your school and colleagues. This is an act that honors their work, and in some cases, their life's work. So yes, try to talk a little and listen a lot.

At one point within the first couple of months at my job, I was striving to regain my credibility and be the change-maker and culture-shifter I was at my old school. And then a new colleague reminded me "Brenda, you

63

A Journey of Connectivism

weren't hired to change the culture of this school. You were hired to be the best counselor you can be for your students." It was a bit of a shock to hear this blunt statement, but she was right. It helped me shift my thinking and efforts to be present for each moment with students, parents, colleagues, and administrators. Could I patiently plant the trees first and then see the forest?

Lesson 2: Find Your People

One of the most critical aspects that determine how well you cope with change is creating a connection with the people around you. International schools are unique settings where the intersection of professional relationships and personal relationships is very fuzzy. You may make deep and meaningful relationships with colleagues that last a lifetime. Your colleagues may also live in the same housing complex as all the other teachers, and you can be privy to personal information you may not want to know. Some colleagues you may not ever get to know in larger schools. But the quality of your relationships with your colleagues has a real impact on how you feel about your work and can also determine how long you stay at a school. But finding people you can really connect with can be a time- and energy-consuming process. It feels a bit like a middle school dance – there are those that dive right in, those that stand on the sidelines, and those that would rather just be the DJ.

This year, I have definitely been on the sidelines, trying to be patient and see who I connect with. It can be a very vulnerable position to be in, after coming from a school where you knew people, and they knew you. Will I like my colleagues and will they like me? Will we be friends or just friendly? Am I trying too hard or should I lean back and see what unfolds? Am I too old to worry about this kind of stuff?! (clearly not!).

Connection with others drives our well-being. Find your people that first year in a new school, and just one person is OK! Get to know and like your colleagues, and invest time and patience in this process. Temper your expectations. Often it isn't the first person you meet who will be your closest friend. Look for the good in people around you. Get to know your host-country local staff, as they can be the most compassionate and helpful faces you might encounter in a day. Find colleagues who are fearlessly positive and will help you be the best you can be in your new position; they will help you grow and thrive in your new school.

Lesson 3: Take Care of Yourself

Moving and adjusting to a new school is an enormously stressful experience. I think of myself as a calm and chill person, but I seriously misjudged the amount of stress I would experience moving to a new school during a pandemic. I would notice moments that I was clenching my jaw during the day. I wasn't sleeping well at night. I felt like my IQ dropped about 20 points. I was worried and felt constant underlying anxiety. My short-term memory was shot. I was working very long hours. I was too tired to exercise. I became anxious about becoming depressed. Wait! *Was* I depressed, or just anxious? And then I realized, it was just an enormously stressful experience moving to a new school during a pandemic. By about the beginning of October, my new daily routine consisted of getting up, going to work, coming home, eating dinner, and then going to bed. Rinse and repeat. I felt disconnected, dissociated, and just not enjoying my new life. I needed to make some changes to take care of myself.

For me, that involved going to the gym on the way home from school, as a planned interruption to my daily routine. It involved kickstarting my meditation practice to include more formal sitting practice. It involved spending more time with new friends and continuing to connect with my family and old friends via FaceTime, WhatsApp, Messenger, and even Skype. It involved getting outside more into the sunshine and fresh air and forest. It involved exploring my new country and culture and learning the basics of a new language. I began to relax, feel better, and work better.

One of the more elusive forms of self-care is self-compassion. Self-compassion is ultimately accepting that you are human and imperfect, and it's good to give yourself a break about it. Self-compassion is not an 'easy out' for mistakes you make, but rather the practice of forgiving yourself for your humanness. Self-compassion is the root of forgiving others, giving others a break, and building trusting relationships. You are going to make a lot of mistakes in your first years at a school. Give yourself a break, learn, and then move forward.

The self-care you make time for is not just helpful to you but to everyone around you. Self-care is not selfish. It's you at the epicenter of a ripple that carries kindness, calm, and compassion to everyone you work with, most importantly your students. It's the foundation of caring for others, which I would argue teaching is all about.

The Skill of Doing Change Well

Everything you need to 'do change well' is a skill. Skills can be learned and practiced. This is great news! Like many skills, practicing is the hard part, because you're going to need to put yourself into situations where you *can* practice. Some situations are safe and predictable, like choosing to sit down and meditate. We can do this to practice our awareness. Building credibility might be more difficult to practice because you're going to have to choose to put yourself in situations that build trust over a long period of time. That requires patience and willingness to learn from mistakes, and this is also why you need a team to support you, and it also opens up the possibility of practicing self-compassion.

So how does practicing these skills lead to doing change well? These skills help you manage the intensity and range of emotions you will feel when you are experiencing significant change. Stress, anxiety, loneliness, anger, frustration, sadness, depression, impatience, and a lack of confidence are all difficult emotions that can be expected during a time of change. These emotions give us important information and are part of being human. The goal is not to get rid of these emotions in order to do change well. The goal is to do them better so that they are helpful to our journey and we can orient towards them as critical information. We can sit with them and reframe our thinking around them to be helpful. A time of change can be a period of huge personal and professional growth if you allow it to be.

These skills are also the skills of connection. When we can embody compassionate awareness in our interactions with others, we feel deeply connected. We are more patient, more empathetic, and more easygoing. We are more curious about what is going on around us, and more open to collaboration. When we feel connected, we also feel loved and valued. We are motivated to help others, and help create a community of compassion and meaning. In connecting deeply to others around us, we build a life inspired to love more, to do more, and to be more.

Advice for Others

Change is hard. And now after less than one year at my new school, I know what it's like to be new, and I can tell you, it's not easy! These are the lessons I've learned this year.

Be patient with the time it takes for people to know your work and trust your judgment. Listen to colleagues that have been at your school a long time and honor their work by seeking to understand the history, context, and culture of decisions that came before you.

Plant your trees and you'll create a forest over time. Identify people who are positive, supportive, and can mentor you through this difficult first year. Look for the people to whom you feel connected and spend time with them both professionally and personally.

Self-care is not selfish! It is an essential part of maintaining strong physical and mental health. Explore things that work for you in your new setting. Self-care ensures you can perform the best you can at your new job and enjoy your new life!

After almost an entire year in my new school, I'm not even sure if I have 'done change well' or not! However, reflecting on these lessons and making an effort every day to nurture them has helped me find fulfillment and happiness in my new home!

SECTION

III

Challenges and Adversity While Teaching Overseas

Teaching overseas is not for the light hearted. Adversity and change are a part of the makeup of each international teacher. At times an international teacher may need to navigate students who have very different outlooks on the world, or parents that have invested the lineage of their entire family line within the expectations of a young student. Additionally international teachers can face racism and backlash based upon their ethnic background and previous experiences. Despite these challenges, international teachers continue to pursue careers around the world and push themselves outside of their comfort zones to work with students around the world.

The third section of this book begins with Chapter 12. In this chapter, Ann Marie Luce discusses "The Many Faces of China." Ann Marie shares her experiences with the one child policy of China and the dynamic between students and parents within her school. Chapter 13 is titled "Cultural Understanding in Bali." In this chapter, Becky Fox focuses on her development of cultural understanding as she learns the ins and outs of navigating a new culture from bathroom etiquette to insurance coverage. In the following chapter "Culture is Complex," Nicolas Pavlos shares his attempt to provide equity of pay within his inequitable school system. Nicolas dives into the complexities and struggle between local and expat hires and the desire to financially compensate all members of the school community equally. In Chapter 15 titled, "No – I'm NOT a Language Teacher," David Han shares his experience as an ethnically Asian international school

DOI: 10.4324/9781003133056-14

educator in Asia. David discusses the roadblocks and barriers that are commonly faced within the Western international school community and the need to increase diversity among teaching faculty and school leadership. The following chapter, "One of a Few," was written by Alex Munro. Alex shares his story of racial disparities that are often faced within the international school sector and the ongoing need to educate others on culture, race, and human dignity. Our final chapter comes from Laura Benson. In "MacGyver Teaching, Connected Learning: Making Social Studies Learning Relevant, Uplifting and Compelling for International School Students," Laura explores the complexities and importance of finding literature to help students expand their background knowledge of their host country.

The benefits and rewards of teaching students from a different culture and learning the different pedagogical and instructional practices of our global colleagues is priceless. Teaching WWII, for instance, to a group of students from England, Japan, Russia, Germany, and the U.S. will challenge an educator's approach to any world event as innocent eyes and ears of students listen to the variety of interpretations and experiences of these students. It is one of the most rewarding and challenging experiences international educators will ever experience within their career. These experiences allow for the development of a level of empathy unparalleled to their previous lives.

The Many Faces of China

Ann Marie Luce

In the spring of 2017, I was burned out and stuck in my job as an elementary administrator in Ontario. I decided I needed a change, took a leap of faith and resigned from my position. In August that year, I bid a tearful goodbye to my partner and children. I boarded a plane for Beijing, China, and embarked on my new solo adventure as a preschool/elementary principal at an International Baccalaureate school. My husband remained in Canada as his career was not conducive to living and working abroad. Our sons were in university finishing their studies. As the plane took off, I was excited, nervous, and uncertain. Still, I knew I had the unconditional love, support, and encouragement of my family.

I anticipated this new opportunity with renewed confidence and energy. I believed the experience, training, and education I had gained as a school leader in Ontario would serve me well as an international school principal. I was wrong. A few months into my new role, I faced failure and challenges with my leadership. My confidence eroded. I realized I did not understand the many faces of China.

Upon arrival in Beijing, I had a government-mandated physical at a location several hours from the school. Human resources made the arrangements for me to go with one of their staff. Kate was a local Chinese staff raised in Beijing who had lived and attended school in the United Kingdom. Her English was impeccable, which made it easy for us to carry on a conversation. During the ride to my appointment, we engaged in small talk about our lives. I shared my background and motivation for coming to Beijing. We then turned our conversation to family.

DOI: 10.4324/9781003133056-15

Challenges While Teaching Overseas

I shared that I had two grown sons and came from a family with one brother. Kate was newly married and did not have children, so I asked her about her siblings. She politely replied she did not have any. I then inquired about her partner's siblings, and she explained he did not have any either. I was surprised. I thought that it was odd that neither of them had siblings.

I continued making small talk asking about her parents and in-laws, their occupations, where they lived in China, and other benign information. I learned that several of her family members held government jobs. When I pushed further, Kate met me with silence. She seemed unwilling or unable to provide any clear answers or details about her parents' work. I wondered if Kate did not understand what her parents did for a living or if she was uncomfortable talking openly about it. Eventually, she moved the conversation to the topic of China's one-child policy.

A light went on and I realized that she was born during the one-child policy in China. This one child—one face was the first of many faces I would come to know during my time in Beijing. The policy was 35 years old and ended in 2015, two years before I arrived. Kate tried to communicate the sensitivity, shame, and silence surrounding this policy without directly saying it. This evasiveness, I learned, was common in Chinese culture. Kate did not want to be disrespectful, insubordinate, or challenge my authority.

I had no idea how deeply this policy impacted generations of families. Jobs, government policies, propaganda campaigns, and history were all deeply influenced by the one-child policy. I began to see evidence of the one-child policy all around me. It gave me a new lens and affected how I entered into conversations with Chinese colleagues and parents.

My awareness of the one-child policy and its impact on generations of families exposed another face. It helped me understand why Chinese parents cherished and protected their children at all costs. Many of our students were only children. They had all of their parents' hopes, fears, and aspirations placed on them. There was no margin for error. Parents felt they had only one chance to get it right, which led many of them to extremes.

Our school children were very privileged and doted on by *ayis* (nannies), grandparents, and parents. Homes were multi-generational, and students rarely did things independently. Chinese families held very different expectations from our staff than foreign parents. Despite our continued efforts to educate our Chinese families, they struggled to see the classroom as a community. Families wanted the classroom to mirror

The Many Faces of China

their child's life at home, which included indulging their wants. Families demanded extremely high safety standards and individualized attention.

Parents did not understand or believe in play-based learning or the risks associated with it. They did not want their child dirty, wet, bumped, bruised, or scratched. If a child went home with a scratch or bruise, parents demanded to see video footage and assumed the injury resulted from bullying or staff negligence. There were police threats, employment terminations, meetings with extended family members, and lawsuits. These differences in child-rearing expectations created disagreement and friction between administration, staff, and parents.

I found myself regularly responding to inquiries from these in-your-face preschool parents about safety. Reactions, responses, and expectations from families were extreme. One such incident occurred in a nursery class when teachers reported a group of parents breaching security protocols. Parents were peering in windows, videotaping, and audio recording the students' classroom. The vice-principal and I were outside every morning looking for parents with faces pressed against classroom windows. We politely requested parents, grandparents, and *ayis* to move off the property with our security team there for backup. We deleted and confiscated video recordings to prevent posts on Chinese social media platforms. These extreme actions of parents and caregivers baffled me. Why were our families so distrusting? What did they think we were doing? Why did they send their child to school if they were so worried? After all, these were toddlers, and learning through inquiry was part of early childhood development.

I soon realized that one child meant parents had only one chance to get it perfect. Parents did not take any chances or risks with their children and held the school and staff to unrealistic standards of care. This hyper-vigilance fostered a climate of fear, strained relationships, and fractured trust. We worked to bridge these communication gaps with parents and put our best face forward to maintain our school's reputation.

Putting our best face forward also meant that appearances, holidays, celebrations, traditions, and ceremonies were extravagant. Concerts were spectacles with over-the-top performances and costumes. I learned just how grand at my first preschool concert. Teachers devoted hours of instructional time preparing three- and four-year-olds for perfectly choreographed performances in elaborate costumes. Parents demanded their children have equal roles and time on stage. Teachers painstakingly practiced with students to create flawless performances and equal time in the spotlight. Staff members were stressed and dreaded concert day. They knew if parents felt their demands were not met, they would complain to the senior administration.

On the day of the show, parents arrived with several other family members in tow, some with video crews or photographers and all with huge bouquets. Spectators formed a line hours before the performance. People jostled and pushed to the front regardless of arrival time or who was in line ahead of them. The goal was to get the *best* seat in the house and reserve multiple seats for the remaining family members.

When the auditorium doors opened, there was a stampede. The crowd ran, pushed, fell, yelled, and stepped over one another to get that coveted best seat in the house. One mother in her stiletto heels fell face down on the red carpet while other parents walked over or around her. No one stopped to help or see if she was okay. The behavior was shocking and appalling. I had never witnessed anything like it.

These events taught me the importance of putting your best face forward and its significance in Chinese culture. It also exposed a dark side that I hesitate to put to paper. However, I think it is important to speak my truth about all of the challenges of working and living in China. Living and working abroad is wonderful and enriching, but leaders do face some uncomfortable challenges.

One of my tasks was to find students to represent our school at events, celebrations, or in the media. In the fall of my first year, we hosted a visit from a foreign politician. I was asked to collect various ages, genders, cultures, ethnicities, and races of students to present flowers to our guests. When I presented the array of students I had gathered, one of the senior leaders informed me that many were unsuitable, and we needed more white faces. "Pardon," I gasped. "We need more white faces?" I was dumbfounded. I thought as an international school, we represented all cultures, religions, backgrounds, and ethnicities.

What I came to learn is that diversity meant American, Canadian, or European. We had many Asians and students of color, but this was not the desired aesthetic. Our senior leadership team wanted white faces.

This behavior was not uncommon. Parents requested these same white faces for their children's teachers. They demanded someone who was a native English speaker. This issue was challenging for me as a leader because the behavior was so overt and accepted.

The Many Faces of China

All of these situations happened in my first few months in my role as principal. I struggled. I tried to understand the culture and context and why my leadership strategies failed. Why were the norms considered appropriate for parents and staff in Western cultures different in this international context? Why were the skills and strategies I had used with parents in Canada not working here in China? Failure after failure, frustration after frustration, I realized that I could use and apply only some of my acquired leadership skills. To be successful, I needed to develop a new set of skills appropriate to the cultural expectations.

I did an about-face.

None of my leadership training referenced the need for cultural intelligence or cultural competency. As leaders, we built school culture but did not understand how culture in the truest sense of the word impacted leadership. I realized the need for flexibility in my leadership style, skills, and approaches with different cultural and stakeholder groups.

This realization shifted my thinking. I approached interactions with staff, parents, and students with a new lens. I thought deeply about my cultural intelligence and its impact on my leadership. I researched, asked questions, and reflected on my experiences, interactions, and conversations. I learned from my mistakes and tried approaches that were more appropriate for the cultural context. I reserved judgment and accepted the subtleties and nuances of the culture.

The failures decreased and I grew. I learned about core and flex values and when and how to apply them. Core values are not compromised or changed. Flex values change and adapt to the context. As a leadership team, we explored our non-negotiables and what we were willing to let go? How could we approach events like our concerts? How were we communicating our expectations to parents? What were some ways to respect and honor their beliefs and values and still meet our educational objectives? How could we build relationships but ensure that parents understood the values and beliefs of our school?

My pursuit of cultural intelligence was humbling. It required motivation, knowledge, reflection, vulnerability, and changes in behavior. My journey continues. During my time in Beijing, I learned about China's many faces. These faces are a part of each new cultural context and one of the challenges of international school leadership. Knowing how to strategically identify and name them to find the right strategy at the right time is the key to learning and growing as a leader within each cultural context.

Advice for Others

Get a feel for your new context and situation. I visited my new school before beginning my new position. This allowed me to observe, listen, and speak with parents, students, staff, and the board. I explored the community and immersed myself in my culture. During your visit, ask for time to explore the sights and sounds of the context so you can begin to discover all it has to offer.

Be flexible and adaptable when learning about your new context. Let go of your traditional norms, behaviors, and beliefs and embrace your new culture without judgment. Remember you are a guest in their country. It is your responsibility to bend and adjust your expectations and behaviors to assimilate into the cultural context. Avoid cultural mistakes by asking thoughtful questions, authentically connecting with others, and demonstrating genuine respect for the culture.

Reflect on your experiences. Discuss, write, and create to make meaning. This allows you to integrate your new learning and insight into your leadership. Unpack your biases, assumptions, and missteps to prevent future mistakes and misunderstandings.

Most of all, have an open mind and heart as you begin your new adventure. You will be surprised when you look back at that face in the mirror just how much you have grown and changed.

Cultural Understanding in Bali

Beccy Fox

For my entire teaching career, I have worked with students from different cultures. My first teaching job was in Whitechapel, London, with a student population that was 95% Bangladeshi. I then moved into international teaching in 1998 and haven't looked back since. It wasn't until I became a school leader that I started to research further into cultural intelligence and how important it is for us to bring an empathetic lens to that intelligence and understanding.

My first leadership position was in Bali, Indonesia. Two things happened in Indonesia to stoke the fire of my interest in cultural intelligence. The first one was that I married an Indonesian man. Thus fast-tracking my need to have some kind of understanding of how he, and my new in-laws, operated. Some of these differences are very obvious, some are more hidden. I'll dive straight in with one of the more obvious differences – the bathroom.

Bathrooms, and more specifically toilets, are one of the differences we come across when traveling. They can vary from the simple squat to the elaborate, high-tech, automated smart toilets. Indonesian bathrooms are quite different from the Western setup that I am used to. I am not talking about the beautiful, palatial bathrooms that are often found in the hotels in Bali, I am talking about the bathrooms that are found in regular Indonesian homes. They have squat toilets next to a large tub full of cold water called a *mandi*, and a plastic saucepan. The water from the tub is scooped up with the saucepan and splashed liberally all over the bathroom to flush the toilet, wash the body and generally drench everything. Indonesian bathrooms are very, very wet. When my husband has a 'shower,' he scoops cold water from the tub with this plastic saucepan and pours it over his

DOI: 10.4324/9781003133056-16

body. In the hot, humid climate of Indonesia, he does this several times a day. Indeed, a regular greeting in this country is *sudah mandi* which means "have you already had a shower?"

I found these wet bathrooms very challenging, and often a bit smelly and unpleasant. I prefer a bathroom that has what is known as a Western toilet, a shower, and a bathtub. I do love a good soak in a bubble bath, even in the tropics. My husband thinks it is disgusting that I enjoy lying in a tub of warm water, in what he sees as my own filth, for more than 15 minutes (or longer if I am lucky). These more hidden cultural differences in attitudes to cleanliness, coupled with the more obvious differences in the bathroom facilities have meant that we actually have two bathrooms in our house. Everyone is happy!

The second thing that happened shortly after I arrived in Bali was that, at a leadership conference, I was introduced to a graphic that I still refer to. It is very simple – a spiral and a straight arrow. This graphic is helpful to understand some of those more hidden cultural differences and is one that both Indonesian and expatriate colleagues found useful. The Western to the point, arrow-like nature of communication can be difficult to comprehend for an Indonesian teacher. It can be seen as quite rude in its directness. On the other hand, the tendency to talk around an issue, in a roundabout face-saving spiral, can be frustrating to the expatriate, Western teacher. In fact, the arrow and spiral can be attributed not only to communication and saving face but also to how we drive, how we queue up, to how we solve problems. I now use this graphic at the beginning of every academic year in a session on cultural intelligence for our new staff members.

Using the spiral analogy to describe driving in Indonesia always gets a laugh. The first time you land in Indonesia and are driven to your hotel, the chaos of the driving hits you smack in the face! The predominant vehicle is the motorbike and they drive anywhere they can find a space: On either side of the road, on the pavements, crisscrossing through the traffic. Cars and minibuses drive in a similar way. There is no giving way at junctions and so it does feel as if you are driving in a spiral rather than a straight arrow. I remember one very helpful piece of advice I was given when I first took to the roads. Pretend you are in a PlayStation game. Drive forward and swerve gently to avoid colliding with things coming toward you!

The spiral also describes queuing in Indonesia. Unless there are barriers to guide an orderly queue, such as at the airport check-in, the queue will quickly spiral out of control. Where I come from, in the United Kingdom, queuing is a fine art. Woe betide anyone who does not respect queuing conventions and tries to jump the line.

The most helpful use of the spiral/arrow graphic has been to explain to new expatriate colleagues and Indonesian colleagues the difference in the approach to communication and saving face. In many Asian countries, saving face is of the utmost importance, and this is true in Indonesia. It is embedded in the culture and can be frustrating and difficult to understand to the outsider. It is more polite to dance around a difficult issue, rather than giving a direct, arrow-like response that might cause disappointment or shame. The expatriate staff member's direct answer can be confusing and upsetting to an Indonesian colleague. I took the spiral and arrow back to my school and drew them on the board to show an Indonesian colleague. She was delighted, "You're just like that arrow!" she declared, "you are so *to the point*!" The Western "to the point" nature of problem-solving can be as difficult to comprehend for an Indonesian, as the roundabout, face-saving spiral is to expatriates.

I can use a conversation between me, a direct Westerner, and my husband as an example. "Could you go to the shop and get some tea bags?" I ask. "Yes," is the standard response, which on the surface appears to be a straightforward answer. I need to recognize the Indonesian spiral behind the response, and depending on my mood, find some patience. That "yes" can have a few different meanings.

a. Yes: I will get tea bags from the shop.

b. Yes: I have no idea what you mean, but will say yes because I don't want to let you down or embarrass myself.

c. Yes: I have no intention of going to the shop but will deal with the fallout later.

This simple tea bag example could be applied when working with Indonesian colleagues. We may ask a colleague to do something which subsequently does not happen. Understanding the reasons why can reduce the immediate frustration. Working through the whys and wherefores can feel like you are in a spiral, but you usually get there in the end.

As Westerners in Indonesia, understanding the importance of saving face and the subsequent spiral approach to problem-solving helped many colleagues, including myself, make sense of the challenging situations they are facing. One example of this was a problem I faced while I was School Director in Bali. A staff member was being charged for an insurance policy he had not taken out. It was clearly an administrative error that had resulted in this mistake. However, this mistake meant my colleague was being presented with a huge bill. In order to save face, save having to pay the bill herself, and probably worried about saving her job, the broker had presented documents that she claimed were completed and signed by the teacher. The teacher was understandably furious, the broker was probably terrified. This needed sorting out so I called a meeting. Before the meeting began, my director gave me a rundown of how the conversation would go. We would be polite and make no accusations. Indonesia is a country in which solutions are found at the center of an inward spiral, not a straight line. In order to reach a conclusion, we would need to ask clarifying questions and see where we ended up. My director, having lived in Indonesia for years, understood the language and the culture far beyond my six months stay.

As I had lived in Indonesia for several years, I was able to help this teacher understand how the meeting about the insurance policy needed to proceed, dancing around the issue in a polite spiral rather than attacking the issue with a direct arrow. And that is exactly how it went. We all smiled, we made no accusations, and we went round in a few circles. I then concluded the meeting summarizing that we had a misunderstanding and that I was sure the head office could sort out the administrative error. The situation was resolved within days, no one lost face and I hope the poor broker didn't lose her job! Without an empathetic cultural understanding of why the situation had occurred and the knowledge of how that meeting needed to be run, the outcome could have been very different.

Advice for Others

Moving to a new country is exciting. We enjoy the differences in what we often refer to as the culture of the country. It is the culture we can see – the food, the celebrations, the clothes. We love the food, we enjoy the weather, and we are excited to find out about

Cultural Understanding in Bali

our new host country. There may be other, visible differences that are not so enjoyable like the toilets. Then there are the more hidden differences that we need to understand, like saving face. When it comes to living in a different country, these invisible elements can be the most challenging and might require an empathetic approach. So my advice is to embrace the visible culture and take in the food, the music, and the festivals. Take some home comforts with you, be it Marmite, 'proper' tea, or a favorite sweet. But most importantly, bring an empathetic eye as you get to know your new home, as you navigate the invisible culture. When things get frustrating here is a possible mantra: "I am in a spiral, I need to be patient, we will get there."

Culture Is Complex
Nicolas E. Pavlos

Somehow, it is already Spring in New Delhi and I have found a comfortable groove at my new school. My wife, infant son, and I have settled into our small, on-campus apartment, from which my classroom and the theater stage are both quickly accessible. The rhythms of the school year have begun to feel familiar, even if we are still learning to navigate the various cultures in which we find ourselves immersed.

By any measure, my first year at the American Embassy School (AES) has been successful. My theater students are committed and passionate, the audiences are showing up to productions, and the larger community seems positively intrigued by what the 'new theatre guy' is doing with the arts program he inherited. The job I have taken on is still daunting, but I am certainly less overwhelmed than I was in the fall.

Shiv Singhal and I worked together closely, and I saw and spoke with him every day. He was friendly, jovial, and patient with students. He seldom refused outright any suggestion or far-fetched idea that I can dream up. His regular, unfazed response to such requests was a subtle shrug and a mumbled, "why not?"

His official title at the school is that of *master electrician*. He has been a master electrician at the school for almost 15 years. In practice, however, the scope of his job ranged far wider than merely running speaker cable and swapping out burnt bulbs in the stage lights. For almost every event that occurs in the theater, Shiv is the only technician in the control booth. He programs and operates the lighting board, while also managing to run the projector. He oversees set construction for the five major productions that occur each year. In the few weeks between shows and concerts, he organizes the sound and lighting setups for outdoor concerts and events. When I am not in the classroom, we regularly walk the stage, the seating, and the backstage areas of the theatre together, noting down items and equipment which need repairing or replacing. Without fail, all of the necessary repairs will have been made within a week.

We sit across from one another on the theater stage. Shiv listens carefully to everything I say, and waits patiently for me to finish my appraisal of his job performance. I fidget, still uncomfortable with the fact that I have supervisory responsibility over staff. I am convinced that the employee appraisal process is just a procedure. A bureaucratic formality that the human resources (HR) office requires of us both. Not only is Shiv's work exemplary across the board, but this form doesn't actually capture the full scope of his job. I wonder to myself whether HR actually knows how many things he does for the arts department.

I smile again as I look down the list of duties and responsibilities, and I tell Shiv that his work is exemplary in all categories. He is visibly pleased, and he manages a humble, "thank you." He has prepared for this meeting. Tallied up on a sheet in front of me are his work hours for the last two months, including overtime. In the last nine weeks we have successfully moved two full productions through the theatre, and Shiv's intimate knowledge of the systems has been vital at every stage. For all practical purposes, he is the actual manager of the theatre.

It's as he's signing the form that he asks if I will speak to Madhur, the head of HR. His request takes me by surprise.

"About this appraisal?" I reply, nodding. "I'll send it to him this afternoon by email."

He smiles a bit and shakes his head in the most Indian of ways.

"No, I'm sorry. Not about form," he says, beginning to look uncomfortable. "About my salary." Here he pauses, making sure I understand. He carefully turns over the paper on which he's tallied up the hours and I see it's a worn photocopy of his contract, in Hindi. He hands it to me and says, "please, can you speak to Madhur about my going to next class?" Shiv is asking me to make his case for a raise in salary. I take the paper and feel my face flush, unsure of what to say.

A few days after my appraisal meeting with Shiv I requested a meeting with Madhur, our head of HR. This will be the first of three such meetings during my tenure at the school. Flush with righteous frustration, I arrive

Challenges While Teaching Overseas

at the meeting ready to do battle and to effect change. Shiv eventually revealed in his appraisal meeting how much his monthly salary was – and had been for ten years. Though I'm certainly aware of the difference in pay scales, I was still struck by how incredibly low the number was.

Polite and professional, Madhur sits at his desk and listens attentively. My opening salvo is statistical and grounded in logic.

"The sheer amount of work Shiv does," I point to his weekly regular and overtime hours, "greatly exceeds his current level of compensation. He is an asset to the entire school," I continue, "and in practice is so much more than simply an electrician."

Madhur isn't giving me anything, his face serene, so I plow ahead with my first question.

"Are you able to tell me when he last got a pay raise?" No response. "Is it a regular increase every year or so – like with overseas hired staff … or how does it work?"

The head of HR smiles with tight lips and inhales, considering the best way to respond.

"Nicolas," he begins, "everything you are saying to me is true. Shiv is an excellent employee of our school and he does his job well – as he should be doing!" He nods with emphasis, then abruptly rises. He locates and retrieves a thick binder marked *LH Salary Scale* from the shelf behind him, and sits down again.

"Here it is: Shiv Singhal, rank of *master electrician*, class 4," he says, pointing to a row I can't read. He looks up and nods as if confirming what he's just told me. A full second passes, and then I swallow the bait.

"But he's so much more *qualified* than an electrician, Madhur – certainly you know that," I say a bit too loudly. "He's been here for … what, 15 years? How can he still be at the same rank he was 10 years ago?" My surprise at this must seem genuine because Madhur is nodding again.

"Because he hasn't acquired the qualifications to move up, I'm afraid." He pokes at the page. "Shiv's pay scale is consistent with his level of training and education. It would be impossible to give him a pay rise without his being promoted to the rank of …," he pauses, his finger moving from left to right, "… of a junior manager." He smiles at the thought.

I try to absorb the details about rankings and class and proceed to blurt my thinking out loud.

Culture Is Complex

"So you're saying there's no possibility of a pay increase unless he gets promoted to… junior manager … which …," I trail off, losing steam.

"Which he does not have the qualifications for, no," he finishes the thought. "Nor is he likely to get them, at this point in his life." He shakes his head sympathetically.

I find myself nodding, catatonic-like. In the course of a few minutes, it seems like the world has tilted a tiny bit. A previously unseen door has been opened a crack and I've been granted a glance inside. There it is, I say to myself. The true culture of the school, laid bare before me. It's a good job for me, but one that I can easily leave. It's a great job for Shiv – maybe the best he'll ever have – and there's absolutely no way he'll ever leave by choice.

Roughly a year has passed, and it is somehow spring again. Life with small children impacts one's awareness of time, I'm finding. The job feels like it fits better now, but then Shiv and I have our yearly appraisal and I'm still at a loss.

Roughly three minutes into our second meeting Madhur smiles and holds up his hand, politely asking me to stop. He patiently explains to me how my predecessor, an 18-year veteran of the school – and an overseas hire – had also come to advocate for Shiv once every couple of years.

Madhur steps back behind his desk and gently closes that familiar thick binder as I consider what else there might be to say.

I glance up and our eyes meet. Madhur's smile is kind, but he seems concerned that I might be taking this revelation of fact the wrong way. It suddenly dawns on me that Madhur has meetings like this every week. Meetings where Western teachers rant and speechify about the injustice of the local hire pay scale. I picture Madhur sitting at his desk listening, endlessly patient, nodding his understanding of the situation. How much of his job is to humor us, I wonder absently? To play the role of *cultural translator*?

I realize then that the man I'm sitting across from absolutely understands the situation. He likely understands it more fully than anyone else at the school.

"Shiv simply doesn't have the qualifications to move up the scale, Nicolas," Madhur volunteers, echoing what he said at our first meeting. He shakes his head with a sort of formality. I recognize the familiar blocking –

he could play the rest of this scene by heart. But Madhur is a consummate professional, and he also knows a thing or two about how to gently manage the various human resources he oversees. He cocks his head, and decides to share some truth.

"Nicolas, do you know what would happen if I decided Shiv should move up to the next step, and I promoted him without any additional qualifications?" He pauses for effect, but the question is rhetorical, so he continues.

"I'll tell you. The very next day I would have over one hundred people in this office demanding to know why *they* aren't able to be promoted. They would be furious! Staff with longer tenures at this school than Shiv – many of whom have been waiting more than 10 years to be promoted – people who have the qualifications but who have been told they must wait."

He pauses to let what he's said sink in. I've begun to absently nod again. Agreeing with his logic. Agreeing with what he's said because it dovetails with what I've learned about the school. The huge disparity in experiences between the overseas-hired teacher and the local hire. How I could spend a comfortable decade teaching at this school and still not fully understand the influence of the caste system on the school's culture. I stand up to leave, and Madhur must sense some of my internal distress. In a gentle voice, he adds this coda.

"It's a *good* job for him, Nicolas – probably the best job he can have, actually. Working here at this school is an enviable job, and he should not be pushing so hard. It could be seen that he is ungrateful for this job if he keeps pushing too hard."

I walk slowly back to the theater and my classroom, angry and demoralized. I feel the embarrassment coming off of me in waves. The campus looks a bit different, as if some thin film covering my eyes has been hastily peeled away. The rocky, uncomfortable truth is that *our school is not only aware of the cultural tension, but that it actually benefits from it.*

The following day, Shiv asks about my meeting with HR, and I lie to him. With a straight face, I tell him that nothing has been decided yet. I say that I will keep advocating for him, and that we will find a way to get him a raise because he deserves it. Despite all that I've heard and seen while the screen was pulled back, some part of my Western, merit-based personal culture actually believes it will happen.

Advice for Others

If you choose to live abroad and work in an international school, your ideas and experiences will always come along with you – there's no way around that. My advice is to try and become as culturally literate as you can. The customs, beliefs, and behaviors of the people in your new host country (national culture) will overlap with the rules, processes, beliefs, and systems of your new school (school culture), which will in turn overlap with your own opinions, ethnicity, gender, and social class (personal culture). For a teacher new to the international scene, these overlapping cultures can often be hard to navigate, particularly when your personal values aren't reflected in the national culture.

My advice is to try and be humble in your first two years in a new school. You may be the best at what you do, but assume that you have a *lot* to learn about the local culture (both national *and* school). Listen closely when local hires and veteran overseas hired staff tell you about how things are at this school. If you do this, you will quickly pick up on the unseen systems and structures that aren't included in the school's guiding documents. As you get to know your school and begin to see areas for growth or improvement, remember this: You are probably not the first person to have attempted large-scale changes at your new school. Like most other institutions, schools do not change overnight. Try and temper your enthusiasm with the understanding that, from the perspective of a local hire for whom this job is his/her entire career, you are just a foreign teacher passing through the school.

No - I'm Not a World Language Teacher

David Han

In 1983, my parents packed up our lives and moved our family from Seoul, South Korea to the United States of America. I remember moving from school to school and quite often feeling like one of the few, if not only, Asian students in class. During most of elementary school, my brother and I were often the only Koreans in our classrooms and neighborhoods. My teachers often sat me with 'Tony Nguyen' or 'William Chen' because, well, we were all Asian. I had to assimilate quickly, learn the language, and adopt pop culture. In sixth grade, we had settled in a suburb of Los Angeles, California which was highly populated by families from Southeast and South Asia. I joined the Boy Scouts of America, became an Eagle Scout, swam, played water polo, and became as 'American' as possible, as quickly as possible. After I graduated from UCLA, I no longer felt like an ethnic minority. English language acquisition and accent were not an issue, and I was fortunate enough to live and work in an ethnically and culturally diverse setting of West Los Angeles, California.

My wife and I are both educators. She worked as a high school counselor in California public schools, and I worked as a middle school teacher and administrator in the Archdiocese of Los Angeles. After ten years in the southern California private and public school systems, a couple of masters degrees, and with two young daughters, we became intrigued by all the benefits that were posted on international school forums and recruitment sites: Travel, street food, tuition benefits, housing stipends, summer flights, professional development funds, international conferences and workshops, signing bonuses, retirement schemes, etc. Being ethnically Korean, we were also intrigued with the idea of moving our daughters to South Korea so they could experience the sights, smells, and tastes of our ethnic heritage, learn the language, and build relationships with extended family. After a year of recruiting and convincing our parents of all the benefits of moving to South Korea, my family and I jumped into the international school world and we landed in Hong Kong.

In 2016, we packed up our lives, moved our family out of Southern California, and landed at two of the oldest American curriculum schools in Hong Kong. All the stories and promises of benefits and expat packages were true. Between the two international schools where my wife and I worked, we enjoyed the expat lifestyle. We were on the road to financial stability. We no longer had to worry about a monthly rent or mortgage payment, and thanks to a housing allowance, we were able to grow our savings, and our cost of living had decreased. Our packages included a tuition benefit for our daughters, and they attended a top-tier international school with all the benefits and frills of a U.S. private independent school *without* the $25,000–$30,000 annual tuition bill. Last, but not least, we traveled! During our first two-year contract cycle, we visited more foreign countries than we had our entire lives (Singapore, Thailand, Kuala Lumpur, Vietnam, Japan, South Korea, England, and Scotland). We have fully benefited from becoming international school educators and we are well aware of the privilege that we have.

There were, however, a number of challenges that came along with being a Korean American international school educator in Southeast Asia. The greatest challenge for me was seeing and experiencing many deeply rooted, systemic, and institutional perceptions, expectations, assumptions, and biases about locals versus foreigners, and about me as an individual and as an educator. These biases are tied up in the cultural norms, regional and global history, traditions, politics, traditional stereotypes, racism, and diversity, equity, inclusion, and justice (or lack of). As a person who does not have the North American or European look of a White expat, I often experience these biases first hand. They fall into the category of daily life, with language barriers, banking, access to comfort foods from home, or missing family, and they also come from daily interactions with students, families, colleagues, and international school systems, practices, and beliefs.

The term *hidden immigrant* seems to capture some aspects of my experiences in Asia, and I would consider our daughters to be more cross cultural kids than third culture kids. When exploring Hong Kong, or going about daily life, I look like I could be from any number of countries in Asia. When my family and I walked into restaurants in Hong Kong, we were handed the local menu in Cantonese and always had to raise our hands and say, "English menu please." When we hailed a taxi and gave directions to our taxi driver, it always took a moment or two for the taxi driver to code-switch from Cantonese or Mandarin, to hearing an Asian person speaking in English. There is no fault here, and what I think is a natural assumption. I've had similar experiences in Beijing, Tokyo, and Seoul, only to be promptly greeted with a "Where are you from?"

On the other hand, we've been turned away at restaurants without even being asked about a reservation or about the number in our party. Just moments after being turned away, we watched another couple (non-Asian and without a reservation) ask for a table and be promptly seated. There were many businesses that seemed to prefer a more 'Western' or 'European' looking clientele. The opposite is also true, and we have also been refused service because we didn't speak the local language.

When visiting classrooms, walking around campus for recess duties, or meeting with parents, I fit in quite well with the student and family populations. Most of the students, while being foreign passport holders, were ethnically Hong Kong, Chinese, Korean, Japanese, Singaporean, or South Asian. We had very few White students or families. I quickly learned that a diverse student population actually meant nationality based on passport status, a demographic statistic for school reports. As a result, a student population could look or be ethnically homogeneous while being diverse in terms of passport status. Other international schools in Hong Kong that offered a country specific curriculum, for example, American, Canadian, Australian, French, British, or German, seem to have a larger population of ethnically White 'looking' families. Diversity was and is often espoused on school and recruiting websites, but the images promoted and the preferred clientele often seemed to be White. The same biases exist with many of the tuition paying families at international schools. Many families are looking for a diverse faculty, which is code for non-local, White faculty.

In June of 2017, I had just completed my first year as an assistant principal in Hong Kong. Students and families started their summer break, our faculty were traveling back to home countries, and most of the senior leadership team had also begun summer holidays. Because I was the only administrator on campus, I was asked to speak with a Grade 5 parent about a report card issue.

She had argued her way past the office staff and manager, and sat in my office with arms crossed, leaning back in the chair, clearly unhappy. After a number of unsuccessful attempts at explaining school policy and various options to address the request, I asked about her daughter and where they'd be spending their summer holiday. The conversation went like this:

"She's in San Francisco with her father."

"Oh, that must be nice. My family and I always visit San Francisco when we go back home, we have many friends there."

"You're not from Hong Kong?"

"No. I grew up in Los Angeles, California," I replied.

Still annoyed, she quipped, "Oh, I thought you were from here."

"No. I was born in South Korea."

"You're not Chinese?"

"No. I was born in Korea, but I grew up in Los Angeles, and went to UCLA (pointed to my degree on the wall). That's where I met all my friends who live in San Francisco."

By then, she had uncrossed her arms, sat up in the chair, and her scowl had gone away. She was all ears, and we quickly resolved the questions about the report card.

This is one of many examples of what I have, and still experience as an ethnically Asian international school educator in Asia. I blend in with many of the local populations, and the majority of teaching faculty who look like me tend to be instructional assistants, or language teachers (Mandarin if you're in Hong Kong or Beijing, Hangul if you're in Seoul, Nihongo if you're in Tokyo). Either that, or you're likely a member of the classified staff at the school, responsible for operations, human resources, secretarial, custodial, or facilities support.

Many of these deep-rooted beliefs, practices, and systemic norms are present throughout Asia and are not unique to Hong Kong. During each of our four years in Hong Kong, I attended the regional East Asia Regional Council of Schools (EARCOS) Leadership Conference, which rotated between Thailand and Malaysia. From keynote speakers, to workshops leaders, and participants in general, I could see and feel immediately that Asian educators were underrepresented. As mentioned above, most faculty

Challenges While Teaching Overseas

positions, apart from world languages, seem to be filled by those who looked White, from North America, Europe, Oceania, and South Africa. When interacting with, and meeting heads of schools, administrators, and other senior leadership members, the lack of diversity was even more obvious. Do a Google search and look through faculty photos of international schools in Southeast Asia, and you'll see what I'm talking about.

International schools have recently received criticism to address colonialism, racism, and lack of true diversity among teaching faculties and senior leadership positions.[1] It would be especially rare to find a head of school or senior administrator of the same ethnicity as the host country of an international school. I have known leadership teams that have made recruiting and hiring decisions through the lens of diversity and inclusion, and with leadership teams that have not considered the value that Black, indigenous, and people of color (BIPOC) bring to a school community. The lack of diversity in leadership has become more and more obvious as we spend more years overseas.

Many of these biases are difficult to shift, especially in the minds of the students and families who pay a hefty tuition for their children to be educated in what they perceive to be high-quality international schools with native English speaking, White teachers. Does a Western education have to be taught by someone who looks like a 'Westerner' or someone who is White? Does a White educator or school leader make the teaching and learning more meaningful? More progressive? More 21st century? More globally competent?[2]

In 2020, after four years in Hong Kong, with political protests, and in the midst of a global pandemic, we moved from Hong Kong to South Korea. Again, we landed at one of the oldest international schools in the country. Our daughters are slowly learning Hangul, and we are exploring the sights, smells, tastes, and history of South Korea. Still, South Korea has many of the same deeply rooted, systemic, and institutional perceptions, expectations, assumptions, and biases that we experienced in Hong Kong, and I continue to see many opportunities for growth at my current school and international schools across Southeast Asia.

There are studies from the United States that address *Why Teachers of Color Matter for Students of Color to Succeed*, and I see parallels in international schools for students who identify with the host country.[3] What would it mean for our students to see more educators and leaders who are ethnically from their host country? Wouldn't there be greater understanding

92

and empathy for students and their families? Could international school curricula move beyond foods, festivals, and flags?[4] How do we improve our culturally responsive pedagogy if we don't have enough representation or voice at the leadership table?

My hope is that this chapter encourages educators of all backgrounds, cultures, and ethnicities to explore international schools, and increase the diversity among teaching faculty and school leadership. I also hope that this chapter nudges you to challenge the recruiters, administrators, and institutions that you meet along the way. Ask about diversity, equity, inclusion, and ask how each of those institutions engage with the local and indigenous cultures of their host countries.

Advice for Others

You are a guest in another country and you have the privilege of being afforded a work visa. Remember that 'your way' is not the only way or the best way to do banking, apply for a driver's license, or make reservations at a restaurant. Many of the institutional practices and systems are deeply ingrained in the host country's history, ethos, and belief systems. *You* are not going to change any of these systems or beliefs overnight, and many of these systems and beliefs will make their way into your classrooms through your students and their families.

Ask recruiters and employers about school perceptions toward faculty who are ethnically non-White, or toward faculty who are ethnically from the host country. Are school families receptive to diversity, equity, inclusion in their classrooms, in their teaching faculty, in their school leadership? Ask about representation and voice on senior leadership teams. Is there gender balance? Are there teachers and leadership who represent the ethnic background of the host country?

For any international school educator, students and families will see you and naturally wonder where you are from. If you are BIPOC, expect that you will have to work harder to establish credibility as an educator or as an administrator in Asia, that is unless you have a degree from an Ivy League university. Unfortunately, physical appearance, degrees, and background are often valued over other characteristics and life experiences that should be equally, if not more important. Whatever your nationality, ethnicity, identity, or skin-tone, question the systems that maintain the status quo. Are the books in your school and classroom libraries representative of the stories and authors of the host country? Who is represented on school publications, social media posts, posters, and banners? Who has a seat at the leadership table where schoolwide decisions are made? Diversity, equity, and inclusion in international schools matter.

Notes

1 (David, 2020; Engel, 2020).

2 (Abdelmagid, 2020).

3 ("Why Teachers of Color Matter", 2020).

4 (Skelton et al., 2002, 52–55).

Bibliography

Abdelmagid, S. (2020, June 8). Black lives should have always mattered: An open letter to Search Associates. *Medium*. Retrieved from https://medium.com/@mabrouka/black-lives-should-have-always-mattered-an-open-letter-to-search-associates-ad8e688f1cd1

David, X. (2020, Jun 22). Decolonise IB: How international school alumni are mobilising to diversify the expat curriculum. *Medium*. Retrieved from https://medium.com/@xoidavid/decolonise-ib-how-international-school-alumni-are-mobilising-to-diversify-the-expat-curriculum-cf3471816fa6

Engel, R. (2020, Jun 26). An open letter to the international school community: Our role in the Black Lives Matter movement and anti-racism work. Medium. Retrieved from https://medium.com/@rachel.engel/an-open-letter-to-the-international-schoo!-community-our-role-in-the-black-lives-matter-movement-c92ba725d93c

Skelton, M., Wigford, A., Harper, P., & Reeves, G. (2002). Beyond food, festivals, and flags. *Educational Leadership, 60*(2), 52–55. Retrieved from http://www.ascd.org/ASCD/pdf/journals/ed_lead/el200210_skelton.pdf

Why Teachers of Color Matter for Students of Color to Succeed. (2020, June 26). *Edutopia*. Retrieved from https://www.edutopia.org/video/why-teachers-color-matter-students-color-succeed

Van Reken, R. (2021). Who are cross cultural kids? *Cross Cultural Kids*. Retrieved from https://www.crossculturalkid.org/who-are-cross-cultural-kids/. Accessed 9 April 2021.

One of a Few

Alex Munro

On my first day as a homeroom teacher in Bangkok, Thailand, let's just say I was more than a little nervous. I never thought in this lifetime I'd be teaching abroad, let alone in Southeast Asia of all places. That's when the internal doubts began settling in. How will the students receive me? Will I be speaking too fast for them to understand? Have my two years in Chicago Public Schools as an educator prepared me for this moment? Will I have harmonious relationships with colleagues? All of these questions and more were swirling around in my mind before the official introduction. The real mystery was how would I be received as an African-American? It's not common to see us living abroad, let alone working as an educator on top of that.

However, before homeroom, the entire student and faculty bodies had an all-school assembly with the customary 'welcome back to school' message from the Head of School. This allowed me to see some of the students I'd be working with as they sat giddy with excitement for a new school year. I noticed a few students, both secondary and elementary, glance in my direction questioning one another on who this new teacher was, and what he will be teaching? Unbeknownst to the students, new faculty members had been asked beforehand to stand on stage and briefly share a bit about themselves and which subject they'd be teaching.

Hello! My name is Mr. Alex, originally from Washington, D.C. However, I've lived in Chicago for the last four years with my wife. We are happy to be here in Bangkok! I'll be teaching year 7 & 8 middle school language and literature. I'm excited to be here and look forward to meeting many of you very soon!

DOI: 10.4324/9781003133056-19

As I handed the microphone to the next teacher, relief set in knowing I didn't botch my debut to the school community. Following the Head of School's closing remarks, everyone in the auditorium was dismissed and we all made our way to homeroom to officially begin the new school year.

As the students entered my classroom, I adjusted the projector one last time to ensure there wouldn't be any malfunctions. If you are an educator, you know the first introduction is critical. It can, and often does, determine the cadence of the learning environment for the academic year. I began with the classic "Who am I?" slideshow presentation with a few points to make: Name, family members, where I went to university – you know the cliché script. But then it happened. The moment I knew would eventually come. I just didn't know in which fashion or form it would take place. "I am from the United States …," I began saying before being abruptly cut-off, "Wakanda!" yelled a student from the back of the classroom. More than a few chuckles were delivered in my direction as I acknowledged the comment but decided not to give it too much energy. I immediately thought to myself, "How could I have been so naïve not to think these students wouldn't be ripe with references to the highest-grossing film ever (at that time) *Black Panther*?" Of course, me being the first African-American teacher to ever roam the school's hallways, and have *Black Panther* come out a few months prior to my arrival, it was inevitable for someone to shout "Wakanda forever" and "T'Challa" at least once. At that moment I knew being their teacher would require more than simply teaching them English – it would require me to share the African-American experience in a way that helps give a holistic perspective of what America (and the West for that matter) looks like through the eyes of not only a person of color but a Black person.

In being called the King of Wakanda on my first day with students, I could only imagine what the other off-hand or in-class interactions would entail. I was curious as to how much, or how little students of this school knew of Black culture outside of the traditional narratives typically found within entertainment, history, and literature. Moreover, I was heartened to know there was an opportunity to introduce historically neglected voices to my students through diverse selected readings and first-hand accounts of lived experiences from either myself or someone I knew. As teachers we have moments that never leave us, for me, this is easily one of them, and I'm thankful for it.

Challenges While Teaching Overseas

On the other hand, we have moments that leave us amazed at how far we still have to go in educating others on culture, race, and human dignity. At the onset of my international teaching career, I was quickly shown the lack of fortitude many international educators were willing to undertake in order to embody a cosmopolitan ethos. One evening stands out above the rest.

My wife and I were invited to a dinner party at a friend's house with most of the attendees being educators or a partner of an educator. What made this dinner party unique was that given the international setting, (i.e., Bangkok) almost all of us were American. The night produced hilarious accounts and reenactments of students doing outlandish things, or one of us showing a parent email that left us all confused, most of the topics teachers expect to discuss when getting together outside of work.

Then at some point, maybe between the retelling of a recent vacation to one of Thailand's many beautiful islands, or the sharing of school gossip, the discussion shifted towards race and culture. For some at the table, I could tell this switch made them uncomfortable as their preconceived notions would be openly challenged in front of friends and strangers. "Wait, so answer me this. How is blackface offensive? How is painting myself a different color racist if I want to accurately portray a Black person?" I sat there stunned listening to this blue-eyed, blonde-haired teacher ask this question with absolute sincerity. I looked around the table, making eye contact with the people of color to ensure I was hearing correctly. My fears were confirmed by the mirroring looks of shock and disappointment. I knew we were going to spend the rest of this evening unpacking the virus that is racism.

After a few of us – mainly Black and Latino – explained the atrocious history of blackface, in addition to the racist connotations attributed to it, we thought this would bring a sense of agreeability to the table. Sadly, the privileged questioning continued. "Dressing up as a different culture is okay. I don't understand why some people think it's wrong. That's what International Day is for. You can't tell me that's cultural appropriation too." Again, some of us took turns instructing this teacher on how wearing the traditional garb of a particular ethnic group is often insensitive and disrespectful. Typically, I would've expected to hear these types of comments from someone who had lived the majority of their life in a homogenous bubble. Instead, these comments were coming from a primary teacher who's been abroad for well over a decade. You would think their cultural-awareness meter would be a bit higher, right? And to think, not once had this teacher taken the time to ask someone of a different culture how they

98

felt about their traditions and customs being inaccurately represented left me at a loss for words. After my wife and I returned home, I sat in bed confused. I began thinking, how could this teacher who has been living abroad for so many years be so lost?

That's when I realized how ignorant I was of the lack of intercultural empathy, global citizenship, and discriminatory viewpoints my White colleagues embodied. I reasoned that White expats must get *it*. They must have all these stamps in their passport because they are aware of the truth. Truth being, the more you travel the more you appreciate that we are all human beings despite the fabricated social constructs designed to tell us otherwise. I took for granted that all educators, despite race and ethnicity, had *willfully* put in the *necessary work* it takes to empathize with others of a different race before becoming an international educator.

After processing all that was said from the dinner party, I began to double down in my efforts to stress diversity, equity, and inclusion into my teaching practice. I wanted my students to hear multiple perspectives and to read unexplored authors. As for the misguided teacher who made those discriminatory remarks, she continued to demonstrate an unwillingness to have empathy for historically marginalized communities. As educators, I figured we are inclined to amplify the absent voices throughout humanity as we ready highly impressionable adolescents to create societal value once they leave our institutions. Truth be told, I was wrong. History tells us White privilege has seeped into every crevice of education, at home and abroad. However, the hypocrisy of international schools with their universal rhetoric leaves me wondering just how long they can continue to keep up the façade?

Advice for Others

Before teaching abroad, you must check your positionality. This means asking yourself how you may be perceived in regard to race, gender, sexual orientation, and more. Specifically, White educators, I'd like you to acknowledge the exceptionalism, both conscious and subconscious, with which you carry. This exceptionalism is often perceived as arrogant and domineering. The microaggressions you inflict upon people and educators of color are racist and harmful, to say the least. We now live in a world where with vast amounts of resources and the ascent of our global consciousness, there is absolutely no excuse for cultural incompetence. Furthermore, it is worth noting that your willingness to be involved with the diversity, equity, and inclusion space at your school will prove to be more impactful and meaningful than the traditional lessons you've taught in years past. Quite simply, *do the work* that is necessary to be the change we wish to see. Your continued silence on diversity and inclusivity matters is being documented by both colleagues and students.

To the educators of color keen on teaching abroad, I encourage you to do it.

Collectively, international schools do not represent a diverse environment despite their efforts to constantly highlight *diversity and inclusion* in their mission and vision statements. Traditionally, international schools have been led and supported by White men. It's important to know the context of international schools beforehand because once the excitement of being hired subsides, you'll notice the many cultural shortcomings found within the international school ecosystem. Flawed curriculums and lack of representation are the most evident in this regard. Given your respective subject matter, you may wish to introduce a Latina scientist whose contributions have yet to be praised, or you may wish to conduct a class read on an Asian author whose writings have helped shape a nation's ethos – and, while all of that is important and should be considered, be prepared to face resistance from colleagues and administration in supporting these curriculum enhancements.

Additionally, the lack of institutional cultural awareness and covert racist comments made on- and off-campus by White colleagues will remind you that bigotry is not attributed solely to any one country. While it is not in your job description to advocate for social and racial justice, naturally, you'll find yourself wanting to voice your opinions in hopes of implementing some type of positive change. Unfortunately, you may be, as I was, one of a few in your school. You'll need to thoroughly examine the pros and cons of this arrangement before entering this unique space of international education.

MacGyver Teaching, Connected Learning

Making Social Studies Learning Relevant, Uplifting and Compelling for International School Students

Laura Benson

In our work as international educators, scarcity generates innovation. Constantly. Let me invite you into a collaboration to set the scene and tell you more about this.

Working together at Pasir Ridge Intercultural School in Indonesia, I sat with the second grade team as we all stared at a blank screen – The dilemma of teaching social studies as international educators glowing at us. Again. A bit of panic. A sense of dread. But we had to make this work.

> Laura, I didn't grow up here and I don't know the history. We can't find any books or stories for this part of the world. We don't have any teaching resources for the host country themes we want to study with the kids. We feel really lost, my Australian colleague shared as we met together in her classroom.

"Right. We are stumped. We love to teach social studies with stories and great books. But we are not finding any and don't know where to go or what to do," our Canadian teammate added.

DOI: 10.4324/9781003133056-20

Challenges While Teaching Overseas

> I totally understand. These voids keep coming up for all of us. In fact, I am wrestling with these social studies resource issues with colleagues back in China and Kazakhstan, too, as we work to build social studies curriculum and lessons with one another. I explained. "We are coming up short, too."

International teaching is often like living a real episode of MacGyver. In the remarkable, but not home host countries where we teach, resourcing teaching materials, even fairly normal ones like markers or math manipulatives, can send us on exhaustive scavenger hunts and continuously cast us into DIY innovations and fixer-upper projects to have what we need to support our students' learning. But this foraging spirit has never been needed more than when we work to design and engage students in social studies learning. Teaching outside of my own home culture and experiences, even as a third culture kid myself, social studies is still the hardest curriculum to develop. As international educators, it is also the most important learning focus because it is the study of people. It's an essential way of rooting our expat students into host country cultures and customs while anchoring and uplifting our native students' connections to their mother country. But developing or working from a culturally relevant, good fit for international schools' social studies curriculum is a constant struggle.

As I worked with my colleagues in Indonesia and as I worked with many of my International School Services school-based teammates around the world, crafting social studies presents a bundle of challenges. Obstacles which we had to turn into opportunities out of necessity but also out of our passion to engage our students in edifying studies of people and cultures and history – their own and those of lands and societies they have not yet had a chance to know – and very immediately the very setting of their own school.

Sitting in tiny primary grade chairs with my colleagues in Indonesia, we discussed our own limited background knowledge for our host country. None of us knew about Indonesian history, customs, government, even holidays. We knew the same was true for so many of our expat students. Not having a great deal of schema for key social studies concepts meant that we needed to develop a responsive stance and pace to our teaching to build background knowledge *with* students rather than expecting to just activate our students' background knowledge as we often do 'back home.' In truth though, because social studies investigations take students to journeys of many forms of *not-yet schema*, our own teaching histories have helped us see the vitality of building conceptual understanding with the kids each time we enter a new unit of study.

With scarcity as our continuing mother of invention, we continued our curriculum development efforts together. As we worked together, I tried to problem solve our collective challenge by explaining a couple of my key launching lesson rituals as a social studies teacher.

> You know, as we begin a new study, I usually marinate my students in loads of reading aloud to build up their background knowledge. And a good number of videos, too. But we don't have any books about Indonesian history and we have just a couple of texts here that kind of fall into the children's literature category. Hmmm…

Pausing to think (always a good idea), the answer was right in front of me all along. Yes, we didn't have the traditional social studies library of books and teaching resources we had each shared with students before at other schools. And we didn't have those we had hoped to use now due to shipment delays (and, in some cases, because we never found any relevant resources to order). But we had better gifts and much more vivid and accurate wells of social studies right next to us.

Taking another deep but excited breath, I offered "What if we try something else? What if we ask our national colleagues to be our living texts, to share their stories and their histories with the kids? To co-teach social studies with us?"

"Agung and Farrel (their teaching assistants and dear friends) would love this! Yes, let's do it," my second grade team partners responded. "We're on!"

And so the expansion of our teaching staff grew and blossomed. With a whisper of an invitation or a gentle nudge of courage, every person in the school volunteered to share something they knew about Indonesian culture, history, customs, music, or crafts. We gained government experts and historical travel guides immediately. The often dreaded teaching of natural resources became alive with the inclusion of our school gardeners and company gas engineers at our learning tables. Many of our co-teachers were our students' parents! Dances and food were shared but with much more cultural context and lots of student journaling and drawing were generated to capture the why's and how's of each feast or festival. And vibrant oral storytelling was woven throughout our learning days and weeks.

Our co-teaching corps grew with the delightful and informative texts our students generated. This bounty of the children's voices became especially helpful because, through the student-authored texts, we were able to develop libraries of mother tongue language text. Multilingual libraries popped up throughout the classrooms and school. Kids could see themselves in these texts and they gained treasured opportunities to learn more about people they perceived to be different than themselves, only to find more connections!

With more diverse teaching teams and the surge of deepening trust and connectedness which came from teaching side by side, we began to ask one another uncomfortable but very necessary questions about the entirety of our social studies curriculum with wonderings such as: *Whose history are we teaching? Which cultures are we studying and honoring? Can our students see themselves in our curriculum? Is our social studies curriculum too North American? Or too White?*

These brave conversations generated thoughtful revisions and invitations to include more people and perspectives. School neighbors joined our teaching. Community leaders offered to help and invited us into their stores, government agencies, and houses of faith. Older students taught younger students more often about what they were learning as social scientists and historians. Parents joyfully joined in to share their expertise about so many different social studies topics along with voicing their own curiosities, which the kids were especially delighted to see and hold in their own thinking. It was so great for the kids to see that learning never stops!

Co-teaching with our national staff colleagues grew our social studies teaching into vibrant expeditionary learning. These exchanges and excursions made social studies so much more alive and relevant for the kids. At the end of the school day, when we had to close our social studies workshops for the day or finish a co-taught community field trip, we heard the lovely sounds of the best kind of learning impact. We heard the moans of students saying "Ahhhh, do we have to stop? Can't we keep going?" Pure joy and the very best data any teacher can harvest as evidence of students' learning and engagement!

Witnessing waves of kindred connections and flourishing friendships between our too often segregated international school communities, in this school and in other ISS schools embracing inclusive co-teaching, we have observed signs of healing our racism, our divisions, our woundedness, our warring. We embraced one another fully as relatives. I see time and time again that the best social studies learning begins and ends with compassion. Reflecting on this with my International School of Aruba colleague, Tess Montenarello, she offered, "We work to give our kids a garden for their social studies heart." Working together over the last years of political upheaval in so many places and enduring the pandemic chaos and isolation throughout the world most recently, we found our way back to hope by being co-teachers in the most expansive and inclusive ways. Each person in our schools has the capacity to teach us something we would never know without them. I am so inspired and so delighted that we opened our doors and that we now name each school colleague as *teacher*.

Advice for Others

Look local. Source social studies curriculum assets from and with your international school community by asking for help and developing teaching partnerships. Host country teaching assistants, office staff, grounds crew, community neighbors, and fellow native teachers of our schools know their local culture and history and, in my experience, universally jump at the chance to join us as co-teachers. Likewise, some school community members have specific passions for social studies topics or themes for other far away locations or regions. Tap into the *entire* community by sharing upcoming social studies themes to gain local and international-focused teaching partners or even guest speakers. Teaching social studies in meaningful ways to our students in international schools means connecting them to people. Let these connections build and blossom with the people of your own international school community.

Stay playful. Play is a vital pathway for social studies learning. Role-playing a market economy for your immediate international community; acting out events of host country history or government processes; engaging students in inquiry-generated debates which they author and facilitate; creating social studies-focused computer games; developing panel discussions or television-style interviews with cultural experts such as local government leaders, community-based scientists or war veterans: These experiences make social studies come alive for kids and put them in the role of actively leading their learning as social scientists by gathering information and insights to develop a deeper understanding of the people and cultures they study.

Move beyond the classroom. Social studies learning thrives and blossoms outside of the classroom when students gain expeditionary learning and service-learning opportunities. Immersing students in local and host country environments helps them to see the relevance of what they are learning, make vital cognitive connections, and fosters the essential rocket fuel for all learning – curiosity. With the panoramic visuals, sounds, smells, and interactions of people, it's hard for students to not get curious as they walk through local markets, volunteer for a community museum, or observe host country government meetings. Give students frequent opportunities to be social scientists and share their learning and voices with the local community in partnerships with museums, zoos, or other local agencies. Your students can serve as local docents, tour guides, and/or cultural experts by writing texts or generating captions for exhibits and artifacts, creating brochures, and/or guiding visitors throughout a facility with their own knowledge-based narrations and insights.

SECTION

IV

Meeting the Needs of International Students
Same Same But Different

No one has ever said that teaching students was an easy job. Teaching students from multiple countries, cultures, religions, and life experiences can be even more challenging. Although these students look and act like students from any classroom in the world, they consistently face adversity and challenges that are unique to international students. The needs of third culture kids (TCKs) are unlike those of students who grow up in one singular culture or demographic.

The fourth and final section of this book begins with Chapter 18 and is titled "A Classroom Teacher's Perspective on Special Education in International Schools." In this chapter, Phillip Allen discusses the complexities and politics interlaced with special education needs (SEN) overseas. As international schools traditionally were not set up to meet the needs of these students, Phillip explores the cultural challenges of working with special needs students and advocating for their needs in a global context. Chapter 19 follows with Lori Boll's chapter titled "Full Circle: An Inclusion Story." Lori shares the journey of special needs students, including her son, and the challenges faced by parents and educators within an international context. Lori shares the story of one school's vision to become an inclusive school for all students. In Chapter 20, Erika Hardy expands on the discussion of inclusion in her chapter titled "Cultivating Community

DOI: 10.4324/9781003133056-21

and Continuity Through Learning Support." In this section, Erika shares her journey of helping parents validate their concerns and their fear of having their child being labeled as anything but "normal." In the following chapter, Cheryl Ann Weekes explores "The Importance of Educating the Community about the Role of a School Counselor." Join Cheryl Ann as she looks at the pros and cons of being a school counselor overseas. In Chapter 22 titled "International Counseling: A Perspective," Rebecca Stallworth shares her journey of creating a comprehensive counseling program in an overseas school and developing rewarding relationships with students. In our final chapter, "International Educators Touch Lives and Shape the World," Monica Dewan details the lives of three students and the unique relationships she has created over her time within the international schools.

According to a TED talk given by Pico Iyer, there were 230 million TCKs globally as of 2013. Though this number is hard to estimate, it is clear that this is a big population. The unique needs of this population of students can no longer be overlooked or expected to be easily integrated into host country societies. The voices of these educators are more important than ever as we continue to explore how to best meet the needs of students around the globe. This section captures just a few of those stories.

Reference

Iyer, P. (2013). Where is hope? *TED Talk*. Retrieved from https://www.ted.com/talks/pico_iyer_where_is_home?language=en

A Classroom Teacher's Perspective on Special Education in International School

Philip Allen

My first experience of working in an international school was in 2003 when I was working as a behavioral therapist in Dubai in the United Arab Emirates. At the time, because of cultural beliefs and a lack of government policy, special education needs (SEN) were not recognized in the country nor in the schools. Thus, schools were not required to provide support to these children. As a result, there was a small number of us who had been employed privately (and somewhat illegally) by parents to work under the radar and provide support for their children in the home. It was whilst undertaking this work that I was approached by a family whose son had been offered a place at a prestigious international school on the condition he had full-time support in class. I had already worked in similar roles in the United Kingdom, so was happy to take on the challenge.

Walking into the school on my first day, I quickly discovered just how ill-prepared the school was to meet the challenge of supporting children with SEN. There were no policies in place, there had been no training for staff around SEN, and there was no way to manage or monitor the progress of children with SEN. The headteacher also informed me that because of my somewhat illegal status in the country, should anyone from the Ministry of Education visit, I was to hide in a cupboard. Not exactly James Bond, but a little unnerving to a young man who was trying to help.

Even accounting for the fact that SEN was not recognized culturally in the United Arab Emirates, the school seemed woefully underprepared to

DOI: 10.4324/9781003133056-22

deal with these challenges. I was curious to understand if it might just be this school or if it was an issue in all international schools.

International schools were never really intended to cater to children with SEN. They were set up to serve English-speaking expatriates who worked in businesses or the diplomatic fields. As a result, they tended to have fairly strict admissions policies that focused on a requirement that children have a certain level of English proficiency and no significant learning needs. Classes tended to be filled with well-behaved students who needed no extra support to be successful in their learning. As such, there was very little need for differentiation. I realized later that this was part of the draw of working in international schools: Homogenous, well-behaved students who make for a relatively easy life for the teacher.

However, over the course of the last few years, driven by a need to increase their numbers and in response to societal change, international schools, or at least the best and most progressive ones, have been making the transition to become more inclusive. This emerging shift toward greater inclusion means that teachers in international schools are increasingly likely to have to differentiate the learning in order to teach children with special education needs.

I got lucky in that initial experience. First, I never had to hide in a cupboard since the Ministry never visited. And second, the teachers in the school were fantastic and wanted to offer more support to the children they taught. I was made to feel incredibly welcome and soon started to feel like I was part of a team. The student I worked with thrived. Sure, we had some bumps along the way. There were good days and bad days. But over the course of the next few months, the child with whom I helped won over everyone in the school, was able to manage his behaviors appropriately, and became a productive member of the school community. It was a huge achievement and really showed that with the right approach, teamwork, and school leaders who were willing to take risks, inclusion was possible. At the end of the school year, my student was offered an unconditional place in the school which meant my role in supporting him was no longer required! It was time to move on.

Keen to start a family, my wife and I returned to the United Kingdom where we had three wonderful children. There, I was lucky enough to work as a classroom teacher in a fabulous school. However, both my wife and I wanted to return to the international teaching world as we felt it would offer better opportunities for not only us as teachers, but also for our children. That opportunity came once more in 2009 when we accepted classroom teacher positions in Doha, Qatar.

Given that five years had passed since my initial experience in an international school, I was both excited and curious to see if anything had changed with regards to SEN. I was optimistic there has been at least a minor shift as the school we were going to teach in had employed a special education need coordinator (SENCo) to oversee the provision of SEN support in the elementary school. Clearly, the school leaders had not only acknowledged that they had students who needed additional support, but they had also employed someone to ensure that provision was appropriate and in place.

Unfortunately, my optimism was short-lived as just a few weeks before the start of the academic year there was a change in the management structure of the school and a new education manager was appointed. He clearly had a different view of inclusion than that of his predecessor and promptly removed the SENCo from his position.

Culturally there were still issues recognizing and acknowledging children with SEN. It felt as if we were being asked to pretend that there were no children in need of additional support in the school. Of course, what it meant was that we teachers were left without support, desperately trying to work out the best way forward with the children in our class.

Now, while I would obviously have preferred that our SENCo had remained in his role, the experience was not altogether bad. The teachers and administration team were united in our anger at what had happened. I think this ire united us as a faculty. The displaced SENCo remained with the school as a teacher and was always on hand to give advice and offer support when we needed it. It was an incredible time, an amazing team, and the experience further cemented for me a love of international teaching, because no matter what barrier was put in our way, we came together to ensure we were able to support all the children in our classes. I taught in the school for four years and, not surprisingly, a SENCo position never rematerialized. SEN remained hidden in the background. As far as I am aware the school continues not to be an inclusive school.

For our next teaching position, we were fortunate enough to secure positions at the International School Bangkok (ISB) in Thailand. ISB is one of the best schools in Southeast Asia. My wife secured a position as a grade 1 teacher and I took up a position in grade 2.

My experience walking into ISB could not have been more different to those I had in the Middle East. There did not seem to be the same cultural barrier towards SEN. Government policies were in place to ensure there was state education for children with SEN. It was more culturally accepted for children with SEN to be in school. The Head of School in Bangkok had a clear vision with regard to inclusive education. He did not want families to be split due to the school's inability to support siblings. He was committed to ensuring that we as a school were going to be as inclusive as possible. This would include supporting children with intensive learning needs as well as those whose needs were considered mild or moderate. He shared this vision passionately, while also acknowledging that this would not be an easy journey. As a staff, we would need support in order for us to feel confident in differentiating for the diverse group of students we would have in our classrooms. The administration team, teachers, and the whole staff were united in working towards realizing that vision.

To be fair, ISB was already very well set up for the transition toward greater inclusion as we already had a fantastic student services team in place. This team included English as an Additional Language and learning support teachers in every grade. There were counselors in every division, a school psychologist, and a speech pathologist; all of whom were overseen by a Director of Student Services. What a difference. Beyond that, the administration team was keen to ensure they offered appropriate professional development opportunities to support teacher efficacy working with students with diverse learning needs. It was incredible.

As we started the process of becoming more inclusive, the school aligned with Next Frontier: Inclusion in International Schools, an organization that grew out of a desire to encourage international schools to embrace learning diversity and that now supports schools as they aim to achieve that goal. With their support, we were able to develop our vision of inclusion and introduce a multi-tiered system of support.

Conscious of the enormous shift in mindset that this move would involve, the administration team encouraged us to make the most of professional development opportunities that would support our ability to better support our students. This included opportunities to attend conferences such as those held by the Special Education Network and Inclusion Association (SENIA), which is made up of educators, professionals, and parents with

Perspective on Special Education

a shared vision to support individuals with SEN. Alongside those outside opportunities, the school also ran in-house professional development days tailored to ensure we were receiving the support we felt we needed in order to be successful. This was the start of an incredible six-year adventure for me.

As the school went about changing its admissions policy, we started to see some very different students walk through our doors. Over the course of my six years at the school, I was fortunate to teach two students with autism, three students with selective mutism, and one student who had been diagnosed with general anxiety disorder. I also supported children with specific learning disabilities including dyslexia and dysgraphia. Honestly, I don't think I have ever worked harder but that hard work brought with it an incredible sense of fulfillment and pride. I was encouraged to take risks and supported with the decisions I was making in my classroom by fantastic learning support teachers. Classroom teachers and learning support teachers worked together as a team to ensure we were offering the best possible outcomes for all of our students.

This was a period of huge growth for me as a teacher. I was encouraged to complete my Masters in Special Education where I conducted research around teachers' understanding of anxiety disorders in children. I became a bit of an expert on selective mutism and was encouraged to share my learning and understanding with my colleagues during professional learning days. I was also given the opportunity to be part of a presenting team at an East Asia Regional Council of Schools (EARCOS) conference on the diverse learning needs of students. This conference is attended by teachers and administrators from all around Southeast Asia. I joined the board of SENIA Thailand, one of more than 25 local chapters accounting for 75 representatives and 10,000 members around the world. Here I was able to help organize professional learning days, share my knowledge by presenting to other educators and support staff.

I was in a school that not only embraced SEN but also promoted the professional learning of staff members and encouraged them to become leaders in supporting other teachers as their schools went through a similar process. We had become a beacon school, trying to light the path to greater inclusion for others. Just as in my first experience all those years ago, we were showing that inclusion is possible only this time it was also sustainable. These were good days. This was how I felt inclusion should look.

In retrospect, my experiences with SEN and international teaching have been a bit of a mixed bag. However, I believe that if you decide to make the move into international teaching, and you choose the right school, you will be joining a community that is becoming ever more focused on truly becoming inclusive. It is also a community that is committed to ensuring that all of its members are ready for that change. A community that believes in the ability of its members to offer the best possible support to every child in their classroom. Are there still schools that do not support inclusion? Yes, of course, there are, but the tide is turning and at this moment I still don't think there is a better place to be than in an international school classroom. I cannot imagine how I would have accomplished everything I have if I had stayed teaching in my home country. I am hugely grateful for the opportunities being an international teacher has afforded me and would encourage everyone to take a risk and give it a go.

Advice for Others

Inclusion is still not the top priority of all international schools. However, I have found there are some schools that are acting as beacons and leading the way for others to follow. If you are interested in teaching in international schools that are supportive of inclusion, do your research. Check out the school's website, read their mission statement, and study their values. Take the time to read the welcome page from the Head of School. Check out the management structure to see if there is a Director of Student Services. You could also contact SENIA at https://www.seniainternational.org/ and ask them which schools they know are inclusive. Alternatively, try accessing school reviews at https://www.internationalschoolsreview.com/ or check the website of Next Frontier Inclusion http://www.next frontierinclusion.org/

The Long Road to Inclusion
Lori Boll

My husband, Michael, and I started teaching overseas in 1992 on the very small island of Saipan in the Northern Marianas Islands. Fresh out of university, we were ready to take on life as educators. With its pristine beaches and glorious blue water, Saipan was a scuba diver's paradise. It was also a fantastic place to begin a teaching career.

Teaching on Saipan opened up the world for us. We were introduced to a new culture by learning about the Chamorro food, language, and history, and we were able to travel extensively. From Saipan, we traveled to Indonesia and ended up backpacking through Bali, Singapore, Malaysia, and Thailand for an entire summer. We visited Hong Kong. Many of our other friends took advantage of scuba diving around the islands of Palau and Chuuk. These experiences made us catch "the travel bug."

We returned home to the U.S. after Saipan and earned our Master's degrees. It was soon into our first year that we understood that the U.S. was a stopover for us. We wanted to travel again and decided early on that teaching overseas was our life plan.

We went to the recruiting fairs and secured jobs at the American International School in Riyadh, Saudi Arabia. Never, in my wildest dreams did I think we would move to the Middle East. Despite several offers from other good schools, we decided this was our best fit. With small class sizes, an abundance of resources, tremendous benefits (we were even given a car!), and a fantastic community surrounding us, we felt we had hit the jackpot.

We discovered desert camping, experienced an incredible culture, and visited countries we had never dreamed of going to. That year we rode camels at the Pyramids of Giza in Egypt, explored the country of Jordan,

DOI: 10.4324/9781003133056-23

Meeting Needs: International Students

and went on a magical safari in Africa. Our school also sent us to a teacher's conference in Istanbul, Turkey. Yes, living in Saudi was truly a dream.

We spent four years there and had two children. We were also lucky to have on-campus daycare for our kids. Where else can you bring your kids with you to work? So I'll say it again, we had it made.

During my first year teaching fourth grade there, I had a student named Dominique. Dominique was a quiet, unassuming, and extremely sweet young girl. She was well-liked by her peers and always had a smile on her face. Dominique, however, was reading more than two years behind her classmates. She had difficulty putting pen to paper and struggled with the written word. Math proved difficult for her as well. I worked with our one learning support teacher to provide the best education possible for Dominique. This was back in 1996, and I soon discovered that the majority of international schools didn't have programs for students with additional learning needs. Despite providing Dominique with individualized instruction and support, she continued to perform below grade level. Soon, the administration told Dominique's family she could no longer attend our school.

I was stunned. How could we ask this student to leave just because she wasn't learning like the other students her age? I had just come from the U.S. and Saipan where this was required by law. Surely they couldn't do this to this student and her family.

But they could. And they did.

Some would say that is a positive aspect of teaching overseas. International schools aren't governed by laws that strap teachers into servicing every student. But even as a very young and inexperienced teacher, I couldn't come to terms with this and never viewed this as favorable. I found myself doing all I could to differentiate and support my students. I couldn't lose another student for the simple reason that they had a learning challenge. Past administrators said that I was *too much* of an advocate for my students. And eventually, this phrase became one I embraced.

We spent four years living in Riyadh. It was very difficult leaving, but we wanted to experience more cultures and countries. So, we went to another recruiting fair and secured jobs at Jakarta Intercultural School (JIS).

JIS has a stunningly beautiful campus, lush with the flora and fauna only a tropical environment can provide. My family and I were blown away by the fabulous facilities and tremendous amount of teaching resources. We lived in a lovely home in a nice community. We had wonderful *pembantus* (helpers) who took incredible care of our kids. The traffic in Jakarta was difficult, but we soon secured a driver and adopted a new lifestyle. In the car we got things done. We lesson-planned or studied *Bahasa Indonesia*. We didn't want to waste our time away.

JIS was well-resourced with speech therapists, a school psychologist, and resource teachers. Students with mild learning disabilities received the support they needed to flourish in the classroom. While this excited me, I still wondered, "Where are all the other children with special needs?"

That question soon hit home.

Midway through our first year there, we noticed our one-year-old son, Braden, was not developing as expected. We took him to specialists in the region but received no diagnosis. Michael and I realized that, despite no diagnosis, Braden was developing language at a much slower rate than his sister, Madison. He was behaving in ways that were not typical of other children his age. We knew he needed some type of intensive intervention that we did not have access to in Jakarta. So, in our third year, we resigned.

We moved to our home in the U.S. and created a life for our family there. We got the services we needed for our son who was eventually diagnosed with severe autism. Braden is non-verbal, has a profound intellectual disability, and requires intensive, explicit instruction.

But our hearts – oh, how our hearts missed teaching and living overseas. We just knew that somewhere out there was a place waiting for us and for other families who wanted to work overseas.

After four years of an intensive program for our son, we felt ready to try living overseas again. But where? Were there any schools out there that would take him?

An opportunity arose in Shanghai, China. Michael was employed at Concordia International School, a stunning campus located in a quiet part of Shanghai. Shanghai is a vibrant and wonderful city. The Concordia community was delightful and fully embraced and included our son, despite him not attending the school.

I became the principal of a small special needs program where Braden attended. It was a nice little school, but our kids were not included at all with their typically developing peers. And the saddest part of all is that our children could not attend school together.

Michael and I eventually co-founded the first inclusive school in Shanghai. It was a small school where young children with needs and without could attend school together to learn with and from one another.

Meeting Needs: International Students

Our children were too old to benefit from this, but other young siblings attended together, and it was wonderful for the families and the children.

I took a job at Concordia as a middle school academic counselor. Concordia did not serve students with learning needs. This was extremely difficult for me as I knew that although it was an excellent school, it could be better. Schools become better when they serve *all* students. Teachers become better teachers, students become more accepting, and the school reflects society. Our students (and teachers) need to learn alongside peers with special learning needs to help them understand how to interact with people who are different from themselves in the future. One day they will grow up and enter the workplace. They will be surrounded by their peers of all ages and abilities. How will they interact with people who might have a learning need, who may communicate in a manner that might be considered odd or quirky rather than simply different than one's own? A healthy school has children of all abilities, all levels. Since leaving, Concordia and other schools in Shanghai have become more inclusive of students with mild learning needs. For this, I am thankful.

After eight years, our family decided to leave Shanghai. While it was a fantastic home and community for us, we wanted something new. Madison wanted one more high school experience before graduating, and I felt the call to go to a more inclusive school.

Teachers who have children with learning needs have particular difficulty when recruiting. In the past, teachers secured jobs, but their children failed the entrance exam, so these teachers lost their contracts. Many top-rated international schools said they couldn't provide differently-abled individuals the resources that were necessary for success, so they made blanket policies to not accept them.

Luckily, this mindset is changing. Thanks to pioneering organizations such as SENIA (Special Education Network and Inclusion Association) and NFI (Next Frontier Inclusion), administrators and teachers worldwide are understanding that inclusion is not just a good thing to do, it's the right thing to do. More and more schools are accepting students with learning challenges. They hire support teachers who are highly trained and who provide good quality interventions for their students.

We found a school like this in Bangkok, Thailand. International School Bangkok (ISB); a beautiful campus in an equally beautiful country. While not ready to take a student with Braden's needs, ISB had a robust support team in place for their students. I took a job as a middle school learning

The Long Road to Inclusion

support teacher. Our son went to a small school for children with special needs in the heart of the city.

One afternoon, while I was meeting with the Head of School of ISB, he mentioned that he'd like to have a program for children with intensive needs. My eyes lit up and my heart began beating wildly. "Is he serious?" I thought. This is something I'd been pushing for years at various international professional development conferences.

He was serious. He explained that he once taught a student who was asked to leave the school and he never really recovered from that experience.

Two years later the Intensive Learning Classroom (ILC) opened at the school. I was lucky enough to be the teacher. We had six children in the elementary school that year with autism, Down syndrome, and intellectual disabilities. These six children were included in the general education classroom as much as possible. They came to our class for intensive instruction in areas where they needed support such as reading, writing, math, daily living skills, speech therapy, and occupational therapy. They attended all specials with their peers. They were part of their classroom for read-aloud and morning circles. Some of our students took part in academic classes that were modified if necessary to meet their needs. They learned so much from being in the same classroom with their peers. They had missed out on these opportunities for years, and suddenly they were included and accepted.

More importantly, the other 19 students in their mainstream classrooms learned so much from our students. They learned how to be a good friend. They learned how to help someone when they needed it. They learned that they shouldn't fear differences.

They learned how to be inclusive.

As ISB moved to full inclusion, other schools soon followed. Many schools in the region developed similar programs during this time and after. A few schools had these programs already in place in other regions of the world. Parents who need to or choose to work abroad now have an opportunity to do so thanks to schools who have the basic beliefs that families who move overseas should have a place to send all of their children, that all children can learn, and that a good school is an inclusive school.

Braden was never able to benefit from inclusion, but I take heart in knowing that times have changed a great deal since Michael and I first set foot in international schools so long ago. If Dominique were attending school now, she would be a student we supported and cheered for as she continued to show progress. She would not be asked to leave due to her learning difference. And students like my son? Well, one day, they'll be walking across that stage at graduation with their peers. And trust me, their moms will be crying. And, most likely, everyone else in the room will be crying as well.

Inclusion builds community. Inclusion is the only way forward.

Advice for Others

If you are a parent of a child with special needs and want to teach overseas, do your research. Not all international schools accept students with different learning needs. Study the websites or reach out on social media. Contact SENIA, NFI, or educational consultants in the region you're moving to. Make sure you know what schools will support your child. You can search the Office of Overseas Schools for a list of inclusive schools.

As a teacher, consider what type of school you want to be a part of. There are many schools out there that only cater to the most capable learner, who can learn without any support in place. They will advertise themselves in that way, so be sure you're okay with that before signing on. It could come as quite a shock to you if you think the school is inclusive and turns out to not be.

If you are a special educator, make sure you know what your international school offers in terms of support. Ask them what resources they already have. You may need to bring some with you to ensure you can provide your students with high-quality teaching with the resources you know.

If you are a teacher and find yourself in an inclusive school, my advice to you is to embrace it. Once you begin differentiating and scaffolding your lessons to meet the needs of every child in your classroom, you will be amazed by how wonderful it is when you start seeing the success of all your students. By designing lessons with your student with the highest needs, you will soon discover that all your students benefit from this careful planning. It's the basics of universal design for inclusion.

Cultivating Community and Continuity through Learning Support

Erika Hardy

I sat in my empty classroom in a north-Dallas suburb, after a long day of wild behaviors, Individual Education Plan (IEP) meetings, goal documentation, duty, cool-down exercises for an emotional student, and teaching my sixth-grade students plot structure using short films. Somewhere in the middle of all this, I realized I needed something different. I was worn out. My passion for special education and students with learning differences was still on fire, I just needed a new means of channeling that passion.

My friend was teaching at the American School of Guatemala at the time, and as I was sharing my day's challenges with her over the phone, she said, "I don't think international teaching is for everybody, and I don't think Guatemala is for everybody, but I think you would love it here. I really think you would be successful." It took me no longer than two seconds to ask for the middle school principal's contact information and send him an email. He politely responded and told me they didn't have a position for me at that time. I felt discouraged at first, but I knew there was something for me there. I continued to email him over the next few months to check-in, and he eventually surprised me with an email that read, "Let's talk." We set up a video call and he began to give me the context of the need for a special educator at the school.

"Look," he said, with a laidback attitude,

> I value your experience and what you have to offer and I think we need that here. I want you to establish a learning support program in the middle school. We've had a very loose model utilizing teacher assistants for a few years, but we need someone with a background in special education to really help us out.

DOI: 10.4324/9781003133056-24

Meeting Needs: International Students

The grin on my face grew wider and wider. We began to talk about what that role might entail and the needs of the students I would be working with. He explained that in Guatemala learning differences weren't openly talked about, and oftentimes were not properly diagnosed. Families would typically get students evaluated around five or six years old for attention deficit disorder or issues with working memory, and then not get them re-evaluated until middle school or high school. Coming from the United States where special education is the law and public schools are responsible for the initial diagnosis, annual review, and re-evaluations every three years, I thought, "Wow, okay. We'll have a lot to do." My face must have looked uncertain because he asked me, "You in?" I nodded and said, "Absolutely."

Flash forward and here we are, sitting around a circular table, datasheets, teacher input, and outdated psychological evaluations spread across the table. I'm sitting with a pair of elite parents, dressed to the nines with flashy accessories, and one of our middle school counselors. Their 12-year-old child is struggling. Based on the information I gathered from the student's teachers, the child lives in the clouds and has no idea what is going on in class. When presented with a task or assignment, they do not read or comprehend the instructions. Instead, they complete the assignment the way they think it ought to be done. The student never asks for help, and often just fades into the bustling background of a rambunctious class. They're a kind, sweet child, but are unable to keep up with the demands of their classes. Their parents got them evaluated for attention difficulties when they were five years old, and have not kept up with any sort of re-evaluation process since.

Before this meeting, I gathered teacher input and did a few in-class observations of the student, doing my best to model the appropriate steps necessary in creating a set referral procedure. If I was in the public school system back in the U.S., the classroom teacher would be responsible for implementing a tiered intervention, taking data on the student and progress monitoring, presenting it to the student support team or the equivalent, and then receiving guidance on next steps to a possible referral for a special education evaluation. It's a lengthy process with a lot of paperwork, which isn't exactly ideal, but it is concrete. Here at my school in Guatemala, processes like that do not really exist yet. I quickly realized that was one of the biggest differences between schools in the U.S. in comparison to an

Community and Continuity: Learning Support

international setting; processes and procedures do not have as much continuity from year to year. However, I remembered that is exactly why I was hired.

Sitting around this circular table, the parents want to know if they need a tutor, and what else can be done to support their child while they're away on business. "We'll leave a detailed plan and routine for their nanny, and we'll make sure the driver knows if they need to stay after school for extra help," the dad said.

> I'll be away in Mexico for a conference, and my wife will be looking after her dad who is sick. It will only be for the next two weeks, and then we'll make sure to be home more frequently to help out, he finished.

I look over at the counselor who is with me, wondering if she's going to jump in and say anything. She looks at me with the same hesitant glance. *What do I say?* I think to myself.

I sit up, shoulders back, take a breath, and look at the parents sitting in front of me. With an easy tone in my voice, I first validate their concerns and their fear of having their child being labeled as anything but "normal." Then, I begin to explain to the parents what support for their child would look like at our school. They shift in their seats and exchange glances as I explain the process for re-evaluation, as well as the accommodations their child could potentially receive in the classroom. I assure them I will do my best to equip their child's teachers with the skills and strategies necessary to service their child in a way that will encourage an inclusive learning environment, not take away from it. The tension in their shoulders ease and I can sense they feel more confident about what we will be able to do for them and their child. I feel the trust they place on my shoulders as they sign off on their child's consent for services, and thank me for my time and attention. As these parents walk away, I take a deep breath. Getting up from the table feels like a feat all on its own. Despite coming to agreements and feeling good about moving forward to support their child, I know this is an uphill climb.

Situations like these happen all too often in an international education setting. I came to understand that it's incredibly common for the parents of our students to be government officials, top doctors and lawyers, CEOs, international consultants, and embassy employees. They rely heavily on domestic help to keep their home life as stable as possible for their children while they're working. Being in this setting, I knew I had to pivot and adjust my normal way of communicating and relating to students and families, I just didn't know exactly how to do that.

I started asking questions to other expatriate teachers who had been there longer than me. *What was the learning support role like before me? What do you think is needed? How can I better serve these students, and you?* I asked the local Guatemalan staff about how to engage with parents and guardians. Many of them had seen and taught generations of families who had come through the school. They were the biggest resource in understanding the families, the school culture, the community's culture, and how to approach specific situations with the right amount of sensitivity and urgency. One of the most valuable things I did was listen to and honor their unique perspective regarding cultural norms and beliefs around learning differences. Their input and voice gave me context and helped me identify what was needed and where we could go.

From what I had gathered at this point from talking to my principal, other administrators and teachers was that our school was never really able to create a sustainable program for students with learning differences because culturally they were barely acknowledged. Our school, much like many other international schools, generally catered to elite families and higher-performing students. Despite the fact that students need to be tested and screened before getting accepted, there are many students who enter the school with undiagnosed or misdiagnosed learning or attention issues because there is no proper education or conversations around learning diversity within the community. There's often a stigma that follows anything that is atypical or nonconforming, which then leads to an aloof denial from parents when students are not performing on par with their peers. So, in order to maintain the status quo and guarantee the most elite educational environment for their child, they do what they need to do in order for their child to be accepted. Money talks, even if the school may not be the best fit for the child or have the appropriate support to make sure their child is successful. This is also a contributing reason why my school, along with most international schools, is just now arriving at the inclusion conversation. The concerns around status and stigma surrounding neurodiversity and inclusion can often be a scary topic for schools and communities to dive into. It's unknown territory for schools that have traditionally always done things one way and cater to such a niche population.

Community and Continuity: Learning Support

Understanding the cultural norms, level of acceptance, and willingness to talk about learning diversity was challenging, but not impossible. Coming from the U.S. where special education and academic supports are law, learning how to work and maneuver family trust with professional responsibility in my new context was like walking on a tightrope. After many conversations with families, students, counselors, and administrators, we seemed to be able to find a balance. And then just like that, my initial two-year contract was over.

Five years later, I'm still sitting at circular tables frequently. I continue to have hard conversations with parents and guardians about their children's academic success and progress throughout the year. The beautiful thing about the present is that now, the same parents in the flashy accessories come to join me at the table. *"¡Buenos días, Ms. Hardy! ¿Cómo ha estado?"* meaning "Good Morning, Ms. Hardy! How have you been?" They greet me with the traditional kiss on the cheek. There are no defenses or apprehensive responses. The anxiety has calmed and I feel confident not only in my ability to share my input kindly and confidently, but also in the relationship I have built with them and their child over the years. They trust me as a professional and also as a person.

As I think back on the transformative experience I've had at the American School of Guatemala over the past five years, I think of the connections I've made, the systems, processes, and procedures I've helped create, and the intercultural understanding that happens when you invest in a people and not just a place. I fully believe that as others come after me in true international-educator fashion, some variation or effect of the things I have done will remain. And I don't know about you, but I think that's a legacy.

Advice for Others

For any aspiring international teacher, my advice to you is to believe in yourself and take the first step. International teaching can be intimidating and scary. You're leaving your comfort zone for another country, another culture, and potentially another language. You're adapting to new cultural norms, systems, processes, and procedures. Regardless of years of experience, everyone is a newbie at first. You're not alone. You are capable. Have the courage to fully be yourself and bring all your expertise and experience to the table. Listen to people who have come before you, and listen to the voices of local staff members to help you better understand the culture, norms, and needs of the community.

Be prepared to pivot your approach to conversations around learning diversity. Your school and community may be late to the game, and if so, it's okay. Better late than never. When beginning to have conversations around inclusion with your coworkers, administration, and leadership, focus on the 5 P's – policy, programs, places, people, and processes. Think about how your school is intentionally and unintentionally being inclusive and exclusive in each of those areas. Culture, mindset, and structures will not change overnight, so be patient. These shifts may take longer than your time at your school, but stay hopeful and confident knowing that you're doing your part and that your school and community will eventually grow.

Lastly, always advocate for your students and their needs. Invest in the lives and livelihoods of those around you; this includes your colleagues, both local and expatriate, your students, and their families. Invest in the people, not just the place. Even if your time is short, it's worth it.

The Importance of Educating the Community about the Role of a School Counselor

Cheryl-Ann Weekes

My time working in international schools exposed me to the major differences between working Stateside versus in an international school. The biggest difference is that my students don't have to deal with the effects of poverty and neighborhood violence on their mental health. When I worked in Washington, DC public schools, Monday mornings were often filled with anxiety provoking conversations about gun violence in their neighborhoods, police brutality, and parental challenges with money, safety, and food insecurity. These types of challenges are not a part of the everyday experience of international students. This is primarily because international schools are private schools where the students are middle or upper class. Their parents have well-paid jobs, so they are financially stable, live in safe neighborhoods, and the families often have domestic help in their homes and lots of privilege.

This does not mean that international students are free from stress and mental health challenges. However, as a school counselor, every day does not feel urgent and filled with outside stressors. As a result, I get to spend more time with students helping them to develop important social emotional skills instead of responding to ongoing crises in their communities.

Some of the significant benefits of being an international counselor have been the pace of work, the availability of resources, and a shift in expectations that guide how I do my job. The best part of being an international school counselor has been that the pace of work has been more manageable. I very seldom stay late, take work home, and on most days, I can take time to leave my office and eat my lunch without feeling rushed.

Another positive aspect is that there are much more resources available to me to develop the counseling program because there is a counseling budget. Annually I get to decide which resources will benefit the counseling department for the upcoming year. Additionally, there is a budget for professional development so I can attend a conference yearly, network with other counselors, go on college fly-ins and continue to learn about the new best practices in counseling.

Another benefit that I really enjoy is the flexibility of teachers who allow students to come to speak with me even if it is during class time. These conversations are the best part of my role as a school counselor because they allow me to teach students appropriate ways to express themselves, encourage them to speak up when they need help, and to learn new ways to deal with stress and anxiety. Seeing students have a light bulb moment, or finding the courage to tell their teachers or parents that they need additional help, makes it all worth it.

One of the major benefits of living abroad is the ability to travel over the school breaks. Working as a school counselor abroad has allowed me to learn about new cultures and norms, eat new foods, and get to work with students and staff from all over the world, many of whom have lived in multiple countries.

Many students in international schools are third culture kids because they have lived in many different countries before high school unlike most of the students we often find in the U.S. According to Wikipedia, third culture kids are people who were raised in a **culture** other than their parents' or the **culture** of their country of nationality, and also live in a different environment during a significant part of their child development years. In other words, third culture kids bring with them an identity that is made up of an appreciation for the different cultures of the countries they have lived in. Their passport is only part of the story about their identity.

Working with third culture kids requires counselors to challenge our understanding of the meaning of home, and to stretch our thinking to consider that home can be more than one country for our students. We learn to recognize that the identity of third culture kids is multifaceted and oftentimes includes habits, food, and understandings from the different countries they have lived in. For some, home can often be the country where

Educating about School Counselor Role

they have spent the most time. One of the challenges of working with third culture kids is that they may start school at various times of the year, thus lending to difficulty acclimating to school culture and making friends. Consequently, they may need more one-on-one support during the first couple of months which requires the school counselor to advocate for them with teachers.

The need to advocate for the appropriate use of the counseling office became a larger part of my job when I moved abroad because the community's understanding of the actual role of the school counselor was sometimes limited. This is primarily because in the U.S., there is a counselor supervisor at the district office who is familiar with American School Counselor Association standards and expectations for school counselors and writes counselor job descriptions. Therefore most principals have a basic understanding and familiarity with standards and the parameters of counselor roles but this varies in international schools.

The most consistent hurdle I have faced abroad is educating the school community about why I am called a school counselor instead of a guidance counselor. Many don't realize there was a formal name change years ago. We are called school counselors because we are trained, Master's degree-holding professionals who are equipped to employ solution-focused strategies to help students with social-emotional problems, family interventions, social skills development, and academic assistance. We do so much more than just help students with time management, organization, and create plans to change behavior and improve grades.

For example, in my first international experience in the Dominican Republic, the school was pretty new and it was their first senior class so there was no formal comprehensive counseling program in place. The previous counselor created advisory lessons from ideas found on the internet. Although it was his first year as a principal, the principal was open to my suggestions on how to implement a comprehensive curriculum and the resources that needed to be purchased to run an advisory program. His flexibility and openness encouraged me to speak up when I had ideas about what practices worked best with social emotional and behavioral issues. In subsequent jobs, advocacy for resources had mixed results.

Other forms of advocacy have included helping my principal understand that the counselor's office should not be involved in the supervision of duties, discipline issues, or giving infractions for uniform violations.

I have had to help teachers understand that students should not be sent to the counselor's office for refusing to complete class work or talking when the teacher is teaching. I have had many conversations about why bullying requires a whole school policy and students should not just be sent to the counseling office to account for and discuss their behavior. These are issues I seldom had to advocate for stateside.

As an international school counselor, one of the most important forms of advocacy you will be engaged in is how the school meets the needs of all students. This means conversations with the principals and teachers to create necessary changes. Sometimes this will consist of conversations with teachers to get students additional time on assignments and to allow them to miss class to speak with you. Oftentimes, this may also include lobbying with parents and student support staff to get students tested for additional academic services when you recognize that their academic troubles are not a result of lack of motivation or organization. Sometimes advocacy will be with the administration about encouraging flexibility in grading policies and creating flexible solutions to address the needs of students who are struggling academically or emotionally or have missed a lot of school. None of this is easy, especially because unlike in the U.S., laws do not mandate most of these services. I have worked at a school that had no formal student support team or process, so teachers did not have the support and the resources to meet the needs of students with learning disabilities. Sometimes it will be parents who say my child does not have a learning disability, he or she just needs to work harder. Those conversations to educate parents require certain finesse, but you will need to have them anyway. You will need to work to educate students about the role of a school counselor so that they are aware that they can speak with you about non-academic issues.

Another form of advocacy you will be engaged in with teachers is how to best inform you of students' issues. I do this through the use of a counselor referral form to collect data on student needs. In international schools, there is often a heavy reliance on emails to share information, which can be difficult because emails can pile up or be missed. Sometimes teachers will want to talk to you in the hallway about a student issue so it is important that they understand that this is inefficient. The referral form is an efficient way to keep track of student issues and help you manage your time. The form will also ensure that teachers understand what types of issues you work with students on and when students should be sent to the counseling office.

It is important to prioritize the collection of data and keep notes on students especially in the beginning when you don't know them well. I found that this data comes in handy when I meet with my principal, the student support team, or parents to discuss my concerns. I have also used this data with the administration to advocate for the hiring of more staff since some international schools only have one counselor for grades 6–12, or sometimes the entire school. I am most proud of my work using data to help parents see that their child is struggling emotionally and agree to let them see a therapist or psychologist outside of school. The case for therapy is made stronger when you have data to show parents how much time their child spends in the counseling office and how this can affect their academic success. These conversations with parents can be delicate depending on the culture of the family and school. However, it is very important that students get the help they need and not use the counseling office for long-term mental health issues.

Lastly, advocate with your administrators to hold meetings with teachers and staff to discuss stress management and mental health awareness. It is crucial for teachers to have an accurate understanding of what students may be dealing with and also for them to understand how they may be affected as well. Covid-19 had brought to the forefront a need for stress management, mental health awareness, and the need for therapy. As a result we have all learned that these types of conversations should occur more often and that all educators should be given the appropriate information.

Advice for Others

In order to advocate for yourself as a school counselor, you must insist on bi-weekly meetings with your principal to keep her or him informed of the student needs that you are addressing. If the school does not have a referral form, it is important to create one and present it to staff at the beginning of the year.

Be creative in your role as a student advocate and work to educate the school community on the importance of mental health awareness and services. Join the International School Counselor Association and other online Facebook groups for professional counselors because the challenges we face are unique and different from teachers. Don't put off professional development because you are too busy, it is important to network with other counselors, stay updated on best practices and new resources in the counseling field. You will need to compile a list of mental health professionals in your area that you can share with parents and teachers for therapy because these can be limited in some countries.

It is important to engage with parents regularly, at my current school we do quarterly parent meetings where we focus on topics like child protection, mental health awareness, puberty, consent, and transitions. Last but not least, practice self-care, set boundaries around your time, decide if you will respond to emails over the weekend, and don't overextend yourself. Being a school counselor can feel like we have to be there for everyone but take time to prioritize yourself. Don't hesitate to seek out help and get therapy for yourself if you need it.

International Counseling
A Perspective
Rebecca F. Stallworth

Truthfully, I did not know what all it entailed when I decided to work abroad, but I automatically had the desire to just do it. After doing a Google search, I found a free international recruitment website that listed so many different countries and the positions they were hiring for in the upcoming school year. My goal was to be an administrator (either a vice-principal or principal) because I knew I was ready. The recruiting agency had a job fair in conjunction with another recruiting agency in New York City. I knew I needed to go there to make it happen for me. It was overwhelming with the number of recruiters from different countries and the many positions that were available. I had three leadership interviews and one counseling interview. The first interview was the counseling one and they immediately gave me an offer. There was a team of two for one leadership position and it seemed they were going to offer the position to me, but it fell through. It was discouraging, but I told myself God must have given me this first interview and first offer for me to accept and become a counselor.

Once I signed my contract, A'takamul International School (ATIS) in Kuwait had their on-boarding procedures list sent to us. When I say us, I am referring to the several other Black women who were hired to join ATIS at the job fair in New York. This connection has formed a lifelong friendship.

Once I got to the school and got to know my students, faculty, and staff, I knew I was there for a purpose. As I reflect on my international counseling experience, I can say it was quite an adventure. Yes, it was my first experience counseling abroad, but being accustomed to the standards of school counseling, I came to the international setting fully prepared to embark on

DOI: 10.4324/9781003133056-26

Meeting Needs: International Students

the international scene at an international school. Lo and behold, it came with highs and lows.

One of the highs from working at my school was the flexibility to work with the students. ATIS was a co-ed school from three-year-olds up to fourth grade, but from fifth grade to twelfth-grade boys and girls were separated by floors. I have always been accustomed to working in a co-ed classroom in the United States, so working with only girls was unique. Although many international schools are co-ed, ours was not. It was more so to appeal to more conservative parents of the Islamic faith. It worked well because our population was approximately 2,800 students.

Since the school did not have a comprehensive school counseling program and I came from a school in Alabama that did, I utilized what I knew and built up our counseling team to use the counseling program from my previous school with some adjustments. The administrative team was on board with all the ideas for the school year. One significant part of our counseling program was our collaboration with a non-profit organization. The organization wanted to increase kindness in schools in hopes that it will spread around the world. This was significant because not many schools took part in it; we were a pilot school. Our students learned applied theater techniques and presented a skit that encouraged being kind over bullying. It was powerful for our students who participated and those in the audience.

One thing I can say, our students know how to have a celebration. Celebrating, I feel, is a huge part of our school culture. It shows how everyone, despite our differences, can come together and enjoy each other. Also, our students are very much into pop culture, from K-pop, hip hop, and R&B, to name a few. They also loved melanin! I recall a time when a group of girls came to me out of the blue and sang Beyonce's "Brown Skin Girl" to me. "Brown skin girl...your skin just like pearls, the best thing in the world, never trade you for anybody else." Just imagine it. It made me cry because they didn't know that I was struggling with my pursuit of leadership positions and constantly getting rejected and the jobs were given to less qualified and less experienced individuals who happen to be White. Nevertheless, I did not let my circumstances keep me from supporting my students and colleagues. I made it a conscious effort to support department heads.

The counseling team collaborated with the foreign languages department and held a World Languages Day and the students were responsible

134

International Counseling

for having their own booths of the country they chose and having all the required elements (i.e., foods of that country, the style of clothing, and other creative things). It was such a great experience! Yes, it was just girls who did the outdoor booths for World Languages Day, but that just meant we could have even more fun. We dance the Lebanese way and also the hip-hop way. It was a great time of bonding, which sometimes you might not get the opportunity for in North America.

What I saw as a concern with my students was the sense of loneliness or belonging. Middle and high school students (especially sixth, ninth, and twelfth grades) are oftentimes making transitions that they are not even aware of until they have heavy feelings of anxiety or anxiousness with an upcoming exam or project. From my perspective, the pressure for high school students to excel and be at the top is high. The government pays for higher education but students have to make a certain grade point average. For sixth graders, the issue is moving from class to class when they are accustomed to having one teacher all day.

Every year I reach out to parents and students by conducting an orientation to let them know about how transitions can affect their child's social-emotional development and what ways the parents can support their child and also my role in supporting both parent and child, but also teachers. I do this because I have seen it in the U.S. and I know that it would be a similar situation abroad. Teachers reached out to me when they felt they were not able to help a student because they observed underlying concerns beyond what the classroom setting can do. From presenting at orientations and working with teachers, it made my role as a counselor visible for everyone to reach out to receive as much support as they could possibly get from me.

From my observations at restaurants, malls, and other public spaces, I have noticed large families not having a single conversation with each other. At a restaurant, while waiting for food, a family of eight did not say one word to each other. In the malls, often families walked around on their phones and did not pay attention to their kids. Not to say it happens all the time, but it happens often enough. It made me think why the students who come into my office finally feel relieved to have someone to just listen to them. When they are not given support at home, it is a challenge to their mental health.

In mentioning this, students also were just trying to figure out who they are in this great big world. To help them, I knew it was critical to introduce myself to each class in addition to the orientation for incoming sixth, ninth,

135

Meeting Needs: International Students

and twelfth-grade students I would be working with so that they know that my reason for being there was them. It also let them know that they could come to me about anything and that it would be strictly confidential. The only time I would have to report our interaction is when they are being hurt, they want to hurt others, or they want to hurt themselves. Once these personal class meetings took place and my students realized this, my door was revolving.

Although my background was the opposite of many of my students who were from affluent backgrounds (non-Christians, with Arab descent, and culturally rooted in traditions), we connected. We all experienced the different emotions life can bring to you at a moment's notice. We cried together, we laughed together, we hugged, and we sometimes just were simply and silently there for one another. Students vie for attention. Their behaviors fluctuate depending on what they are going through, just like it does for us adults. Being able to give my students a safe space to express themselves without judgment really built their confidence. Things they could not share with their parents for fear of punishment, they were able to get it off their chests and go through the school day without a heavy heart.

I specifically remember a student who came into my office and asked me "Can I hug you?" I worked with this student regularly and for this student to do this showed me that they were making gains and that hug meant everything. By listening and showing my empathy, it made a world of difference in the lives of students. As I recall, I was able to be more interactive with my students in the international scene. Parents, for the most part, were receptive to trying to get the help their child needed, but they did not follow through and brush off a lot of the seriousness of their child's concerning behavior. I had to tell myself as long as I can give them the needed support while they are at school, I am doing something for their good. The highs of being an international counselor focused on the social-emotional aspect of students was being able to be their safe space to express themselves with no judgment. Society wanted them a certain way and they just wanted to be who they are and that divide was a struggle for students, but I felt that them being able to discuss it out loud helped them to feel better about themselves and somewhat find a middle ground between social needs and their needs.

As I have stated before, I had more highs than lows as a counselor working internationally, but the lows were tough. I realized that not every

International Counseling

school has a strong counseling program, but we do what we can and hope that administrators support what we do. When you are having to battle culture, ideologies, religion, and an intrinsic fear of being fired for doing what is right, it makes working in certain schools difficult. At one point, I found myself having to educate the school leaders on what counseling is and what protocols and procedures were needed, and how it should be handled. From child abuse to suicidal ideation, there are protocols in place. Unfortunately, there was not much support in following through because people feared being blackballed or attacked in some way for reporting these instances. Some countries have strong mental health organizations and programs and some do not. Not every country has protocols in place to protect students. Hopefully, over time improvements will be made.

Advice for Others

Working as a counselor at an international school is a great experience overall, and although there are several areas to take into consideration when making a decision to work abroad, it can be worthwhile. It is important to be mindful of the location, the roles of a school counselor at the school you will be working in, mental health resources available in that country, and other pertinent information to provide the best school counseling program.

One point to say is, what looks good on the outside is not necessarily good on the inside. A country may be rich in the monetary sense but lack the richness in mental health and well-being. Meaning, look into the country you are interested in working and see what mental health programs and resources they have and what is lacking. Some countries believe mental health is not a concern, but you will more than likely experience the opposite. Of course, you cannot control what others do, but you can help students blossom while in your care. When looking for international jobs, please do not be afraid to ask tough questions. Have a list of questions and add to it the more you look into the schools that catch your attention.

What I cannot stress enough, please do research into the schools you are interested in because recruiters and the human resources team have the gift of charisma. Also, trust your instincts. If recruiters or hiring managers brush off your questions to make it seem as though there is nothing to worry about, take that as a possible red flag. As a counselor, ask deep questions about what their policies are regarding mental health concerns, child abuse/neglect, suicide prevention, and other critical areas. It might be taboo in certain countries, which does a disservice to our students. Children everywhere are struggling to feel good on the inside so that they can live life fully without negative self-talk or feeling unsafe. Again, do some research and determine what is best for you.

International Educators Touch Lives and Shape the World

Monika Dewan

In an international context, it is a unique and special privilege to teach diverse learners from various nationalities, where we can learn a lot from each other's experiences. I enjoy every moment teaching students irrespective of their ethnicity, and having a common language barrier. I came to learn that it is imperative to ensure I respect and treat each with a fair approach, and I do my best to inculcate these traits in my students. Three of my students come to mind, Alisha, Amish, and Adhish, all three from different cultures.

 Alisha

Alisha was a new student who came from Korea to join American Embassy School in New Delhi, India. This was her first overseas travel and move. We had other students in the class from America, U.K., Israel, India, Japan, and Australia. All students were experienced at some point to be very new to the school and the class on their first day, and hence understood what it feels like to arrive in a new set-up at an international school. We welcomed Alisha and were very happy to have her join our class.

This is a reflection on one of the best lessons I've ever taught when Alisha joined our school and came to PE for the first time. With my grade four soccer unit, I was consciously stressing inculcating social traits like being respectful and tolerant. Throughout the unit, students were working with each other, yet, at the same time improving their skills and the game.

Towards the end of the unit, we had Alisha join us. She was completely new to soccer. She was a beginner English as an Additional Language (EAL)

DOI: 10.4324/9781003133056-27

learner. My assistant worked on introducing soccer skills to her, and when we were about to play the game, she was added to one of the teams. The students were following all the rules, as explained. It was just like any regular game with players playing their positions, until this event occurred, which changed my opinion regarding the class, and made this my most special lesson.

Alisha was new to our school, new to the game of soccer, with beginner linguistic skills in English. Nevertheless, she stopped the ball, turned around, and shot in the goal. Suddenly, one team started rejoicing spontaneously, "Yeah! We scored." The other team realizes that she was in the offside position. That was clearly visible. To my surprise, the moment I blew my whistle, all students sat down for a quick discussion to understand the event. There was a moment of silence. I wanted to observe how my students would react. I could see them looking at each other, analyzing that this was probably Alisha's first-ever contact with a soccer ball. They realized that calling an offside for a beginner-player might not be in the best interest of the student. The entire class decided not to call it offside, as this would disturb the sentiments of a new player. They exhibited extremely respectful and tolerant behavior, by not being bothered about the score and just playing on. I was touched and completely impressed. I felt positive and it was a very emotional moment for me to observe their spontaneous reaction.

The student very innocently asked me, "Dr. Dewan. What did I do?" Everybody responded rejoicing, "Congratulations! You scored. Let's play on." Instead of making a fuss about it, they applauded her efforts, gave her a high five, and said, "Good job." At the same time, they pointed to her to shoot in the other goal from next time. She nodded, smiled, and understood.

This was a rare moment of eternal satisfaction and happiness for me. I was so moved by their gesture and understanding of these big terms at such a tender age. This brings out the in-depth learning of respect and tolerance by our students and how well they internalize what they are taught. I was moved by the maturity in the development of traits like tolerance and open-mindedness of my students. Their respectful approach to this whole episode just made me realize, focusing on these social traits, the whole unit was really worth it. I can say this was my best lesson, as it laid an impact forever on my new student, my entire class, and particularly me as an educator. The innocence that is prevalent amongst international students comes out beautifully here, and Alisha's story shows a glimpse of it.

I wish to have a long-term impact on the lives of the students I teach, such that I influence their lives, guiding them to be worthy, devoted, and dedicated members of society. I strongly believe in Henry Ward Beecher's statement, "That energy which makes a child hard to manage is the energy which afterward makes him a manager of life." My inspiration is the potential of children to learn and their everlasting energy levels. If students' energy is channelized in correct and positive directions, with encouragement and motivation, the next generation can reach great heights. We educators must focus on building responsible and compassionate students through our teachings. Teaching students of multiple nationalities under one roof and who belong to different cultures is a challenging yet exciting experience, and the immense satisfaction received as an international educator is a beautiful feeling. This experience is unique to international schools.

Amish

Amish was a middle school student from America, studying at American Embassy School in New Delhi, India. An expatriate, whose parents were diplomats, Amish deeply impacted my teaching style. He was in my health education class, which consisted of students of various nationalities such as Japanese, Korean, Swedish, Australian, Indian, Chinese, and American, as expected in an international school. While I had a few English language learners, there were a few native English speakers. Amish, a native English speaker from America, was least interested in the health class and conveyed repeatedly that he did not wish to be taught by a teacher from the host country that he lived in, especially as he was studying in an international school. He wanted to be taught by a native English teacher only!

He had a few medical issues and those led to some behaviors which were usually unacceptable. He would run out of the classroom without informing or asking permission whenever he wanted. Being a playful boy, he would have plenty of ideas to disrupt the learning environment, and would often come well prepared with ideas for spoiling the decorum of the class. His continual provocation of his classmates by making offensive remarks, banging the desk or the door, and switching off the lights was

Meeting Needs: International Students

very distracting for us, yet, normal for him. He thought he knew everything about health as his parents were in the field of medicine, and he vocally expressed that the class was a waste of his time. Every time he was placed in a group, he would ask one of the group members to leave because he did not like them due to their ethnicity. He could easily upset a group member who was from India, and students did not feel comfortable with this behavior. Not only this, his treatment towards host country educators was painful too. He expressed that all the host country teachers spoke gibberish. He exhibited disrespectful behavior towards the school administrators as well.

He tested my patience, which I have in abundance, and reminded me of the quote by W.C. Sellar and R.J. Yeatman, "For every person wishing to teach, there are thirty not wanting to be taught." I sometimes jokingly thought to myself, that this one student of mine, was equal to 30 students!

Amish made it very difficult for me to teach him. He accepted foreigners as his teachers very easily. I, on my part, continued to explain to him about equality, respecting the learning process, and understanding that all children in his class were demonstrating exemplary tolerance. These are traits we must possess. I felt very supported as I was in regular communication with his parents and their understanding was a great pillar of strength as I continued teaching Amish. His parents and I used certain interventions to encourage and inculcate appropriate behaviors in Amish. We shared research with Amish about treating other cultures and people with respect. I had a strong support system in our school where there was administrator and counselor support. We reviewed research reports about the understanding that respect for other cultures and other people should be a core value that is non-negotiable at school, home, or anywhere else.

Once I was unwell, and it was Amish who identified immediately and asked me if I needed anything and if he could help me. He offered to take me to the health office. I had tears trickling down my cheeks. He was extremely concerned and worried. They were tears of joy. Where else could I get better satisfaction than that moment? To observe that level of concern by Amish was a rewarding experience. Such growth in him was certainly accompanied by hard work, dedication, and sincere commitment. From that day on, I was teaching a different Amish.

At the beginning of my career, I really wished that kids came with a manual of instructions. I have realized that each individual is unique and has an individual learning style. With experience and practice, one attains

Touching Lives and Shaping the World

intellectual maturity and an improvement in one's performance. An international school gives us the best opportunity and a supportive environment to teach diverse learners, and helps them develop empathy and compassion, and I love to see students like Amish and others imbibe these traits.

Adhish

Below is a letter I received from a student named Adhish a few years ago. Adhish was a fifth-grade Australian student at American Embassy School in New Delhi, India, who always participated as desired in the class.

Dear Mrs. Dewan,

Hello. I am Adhish, and you were my PE teacher in Grade 5. I hope you remember me! I am from Mr. John's class of 2005, in which we had Alon, Peter, Samantha, Harry, and Luke.

We all were such a mischievous lot to deal with. I was always impressed with how diligently and politely you dealt with us.

With your blessings and guidance, I am a director of a dance company now. I really wish we had a PE Teacher like you in every school. I wish to write that the traits you built within us, have helped me come up a long way in life. I value you as a teacher and am thankful. I always looked forward to PE class, and the best memories I have from school are from PE. The learning and fun we had were memorable and unforgettable. You taught us not just physical skills, but also touched every other aspect we needed to be able to become successful global citizens. The holistic development and nurturing you provided were a match to none.

I wish to thank you from the bottom of my heart and am looking forward to my visit to India when I can see you again.

Sincere regards and gratitude,

Adhish

This letter touched my heart and moved me immensely. I feel my contributions of teaching international students over the years paid off well when I have touched lives and shaped them better. I am happy to see my responsible, compassionate learners, trust and value each other and contribute their bit to make the world a better place. I believe that the diversity in an international school enriches us. We become passionate about learning, while we maintain attributes such as resilience, empathy, and respect for others in an international school. It is indeed an honor to teach human hearts!

Advice for Others

As a locally-based teacher in an international school, I urge educators across the world to explore teaching at an international school. It will really be worth the effort. While we get immense opportunities to grow and develop ourselves professionally, we also get support, while effecting a deep impact on the lives of our students. The intercultural environment that depicts a global community provides inclusive and holistic opportunities to develop students and educators. The international school set-up provides live experiences to educate our students regarding differences of opinions and accepting situations gracefully. We understand that we are a valuable part of a whole, and we are connected. It is a privilege as an international educator to be a contributor to shaping the future world. The seeds of learning we sow are dispersed in different parts of the world, due to the transient nature of our student population. The fragrance of positive values eventually spreads all over. With this vision and passion, I encourage all international educators to keep delivering their best. The challenges and struggles related to teaching diverse learners come with strong support systems. You will never feel alone or isolated. As resilient lifelong learners, I advise all international educators to stay focused on our goal of spreading awareness and compassion. We have the power to change the world for the better!

Appendix A
Common Vocabulary Used within International Schools

Types of International Schools

1. **Government schools.** Although a multitude of schools label themselves international, the roots of the international school system are closely aligned with the United States government. Government schools include (a) embassy schools, (b) Department of Defense Dependent Schools (DoDDS), and (c) Department of State Schools. The interconnected nature of these three models can create confusion for educators and parents searching for an international education for their children but a unifying factor is the leadership within these organizations mirrors the U.S. system and they are beholden to U.S. regulations regarding testing and standards. These schools may have less autonomy than the below models regarding their governing body, accreditation, curriculum, and sources for funding.

    a. **Embassy schools**: The genesis of embassy schools was the need to educate the children of diplomats serving overseas. Enrollment is generally limited to children whose parents are on diplomatic missions, although exceptions exist depending on the bylaws of the embassy school.

    b. **Department of Defense Dependent Schools (DoDDS)**: Schools under the direction of the DoDDS fall under the leadership of the U.S. Department of State Office of Overseas

Appendix A

Schools and they are solely composed of American children that have one or both parents deployed overseas.

c. **Department of State Schools:** Department of State schools are similar to the above models however enrollment includes, "children of employees of other government agencies and private businesses, as well as host-country and third country nationals" (Brown, 2000, pp. 43–44).

2. **For-profit, corporate, proprietary, franchise, and niche schools.** The umbrella terminology of international schools can be expanded to include niche schools which include for-profit, corporate, proprietary, and franchise schools. Bunnell (2008) argued that, "International schooling is moving from being an elite niche market to being an elite mass one" (p. 223). Recent attention has focused on organizations that are operating chains of international schools; these may include for-profit (e.g., Cognita, GEMS Education, Nord Anglia Education), corporate type (e.g., Saudi Aramco Expatriate Schools, Oberoi International), proprietary (e.g., GEMS, Oberoi), and franchise schools (e.g., Dulwich, Harrow) (Bunnell, 2008). The lack of framework and distinct categories for these schools creates a large amount of crossover in distinguishing these schools from one another. These school models are often owned by companies that operate in several countries and Waterson (2016) classified these models as transnational corporations. There is a growing market within the for-profit sector of international education. The autonomy of niche schools is dependent upon the governing body, which can have a direct impact upon accreditation, curriculum, and sources of funding.

3. **International boarding schools.** Some international schools also function as boarding schools. Two models of boarding are common. Some boarding programs draw from a nearby urban area sufficiently far to make daily commuting unrealistic. These students spend the weekend with their parents returning to the school to board during the week. The more traditional boarding programs draw from very large regions making any form of commuting unrealistic. In addition to specialized boarding facilities, food services and medical services must also be provided.

Appendix A

Boarding programs also have trained pastoral and supervisory personnel to care for the students outside of the classroom.

4. **Non-profit and not-for-profit schools.** Non-profit and not-for-profit international schools are composed of expatriates from multinational companies, government organizations, NGOs, and private companies. Nonprofit and not-for-profit international schools may also include cooperative community schools, foundation schools, contract schools, and religious schools. Non-profit and not-for-profit have autonomy over their governing body, accreditation, curriculum, and funding sources. Currently, nonprofit and not-for-profit schools are the most frequently found model of international school.

Curriculum & Standards

- **Advanced Placement (AP):** A U.S. program created by the College Board which offers college-level curricula and exams to high school students.
- **American Education Reaches Out (AERO):** A curricular framework supported by the U.S. State Department's Office of Overseas Schools and the Overseas Schools Advisory Council.
- **College, Career, and Civic Life (C3):** A set of standards for social studies that are aligned to the Common Core.
- **Collaborative for Academic, Social, and Emotional Learning (CASEL):** A set of learning standards designed for school counseling programs.
- **Common Core State Standards (CCSS):** A set of learning standards designed to provide teachers with a guideline of what skills and knowledge students need so that they can prepare students for future success.
- **Common Ground Collaborative (CGC):** An alternative to traditional 'curriculum' designs – a coherent Learning Ecosystem that connects learning, leading, teaching and assessing into one simple, systemic approach.
- **International Baccalaureate (IB):** Offers a continuum of international education through four programs that cover all stages of

147

Appendix A

a student's education from ages 3 to 19. These include the Primary Years Programme (PYP), Middle Years Programme (MYP), Diploma Programme (DP), and Career-Related Programme (CP).

- **National Core Arts Standards (NCCAS):** A set of learning standards for dance, media arts, music, theatre, and visual arts. They are based on the artistic processes of Creating; Performing/Producing/Presenting; Responding; and Connecting.

- **Next Generation Science Standards (NGSS):** Science learning standards and the science arm of the Common Core Learning Standards.

- **Society of Health and Physical Educators (SHAPE):** Standards and grade-level outcomes for K-12 physical education.

Common Terminology Related to Instruction & Pedagogy

- **Anti-bias/Anti-racism:** An approach that focuses on dismantling systemic racism.

- **Augmented and virtual reality:** Virtual reality immerses users in a completely different world, while augmented reality layers virtual elements over a real-world view.

- **Backward design:** Designing curriculum backward by starting with the outcomes, assessments, and goals first.

- **Black, Indigenous, People of Color (BIPOC):** Term used to describe racial minorities.

- **Bring your own device (BYOD):** Refers to a program in which students are each responsible for bringing their own device to school (i.e., laptops, ChromeBook, iPads).

- **Creativity, Activity, Service (CAS):** Hours that are a mandatory component of the IB Diploma Programme.

- **Co-teaching:** When two or more teachers work together with groups of students; sharing the planning, organization, delivery, and assessment of instruction, as well as the physical space.

148

Appendix A

- **Culturally responsive teaching:** Teaching competencies and reflections that help educators self-appraise, set goals, have critical conversations around DEIJ topics.
- **Dependents:** Refers to the amount of dependents the school will need to provide visas, tuition, and housing for within the host country of the school.
- **Diversity, equity, inclusion, and justice (DEIJ):** Most formally used nomenclature to describe efforts and initiatives around diversity, equity, inclusion, and justice.
- **Design thinking:** The design thinking process, from Stanford University, involves five steps: empathize, define, ideate, prototype, and test.
- **Differentiated instruction:** Differentiation means tailoring instruction to meet individual needs. This may include teachers differentiating content, process, products, or the learning environment with the use of ongoing assessment and flexible grouping.
- **Distant learning:** Also called distance education, virtual school, remote learning, e-learning, hybrid, and online learning, are forms of education in which the main elements include physical separation of teachers and students during instruction and the use of various technologies to facilitate student-teacher and student-student communication.
- **English as an Additional Language (EAL):** A common term used for English as a Second Language (ESL) and English for Speakers of Other Languages (ESOL).
- **English Language Arts (ELA):** A common term for literacy subjects.
- **Flexible seating:** The idea behind the trend is to create a space which allows for choice, where all students can find a place where they feel comfortable. Some examples of alternative seating include bean bag chairs, exercise balls, bar stools and high top tables, sofas, armchairs, floor cushions, plus traditional tables and chairs.
- **Flipped learning:** A pedagogical approach in which direct instruction moves from the group learning space to the individual learning space, and the resulting group space is transformed into a dynamic, interactive learning environment where the educator guides students as they apply concepts and engage creatively in the subject matter.

149

Appendix A

- **Formative assessment:** Formative assessment is used to evaluate student learning at the beginning or during a unit. This information is used to inform instruction and provides information for the teacher and learner about what needs to be covered/adjusted.

- **Guided reading:** Guided reading is a strategy that teachers use to help students become great readers. The teacher's role is to provide support to a small group of students by using a variety of reading strategies to guide them to become successful in reading. This strategy is primarily associated with primary grades but can be adapted in all grade levels.

- **Habits of mind (HOM):** An identified set of 16 problem solving, life related skills, necessary to effectively operate in society and promote strategic reasoning, insightfulness, perseverance, creativity, and craftsmanship.

- **Head of school (HOS):** Serves as the director or superintendent of the school.

- **Host country:** The country where a person or school is based.

- **Humanities:** The combination of English language arts and social studies into one subject/content area. This is a common practice found in several international secondary schools.

- **Inclusive education:** An approach to educating children with learning difficulties and disabilities with all students under one roof regardless of their abilities.

- **Learning management system (LMS):** Software that is used by schools to track grades, deliver curriculum, offer or evaluate courses, etc.

- **Local hire:** Educators and staff who have been hired within the host country and/or permanently reside within the host country of the school.

- **Makerspace:** A collaborative workspace that is sometimes high-tech and sometimes not – coding, 3D modeling, robotics, woodworking, etc.

- **Overseas hire:** Educators and staff who have been hired outside the host country and/or do not permanently reside within the host country of the school.

- **Project-based learning (PBL):** A collaborative learning method that addresses real-world problems, emphasizing critical thinking and

Appendix A

problem-solving skills. Starting with a challenging question or issue facing the community, students are given voice and choice in how they will solve the problem and evaluate their solution.

- **Peer assessment:** Peer assessment refers to when students of equal status assess each other's work.
- **Personal learning network (PLN) or professional learning community (PLC):** Refers to work colleagues or education connections made on social media or through organizations.
- **Positive education:** Positive education brings positive psychology to the classroom. It emphasizes our strengths and examines what makes us successful and happy. Teaching character and well-being, positive education revives education, as the brain flourishes on happiness and positivity.
- **Standards-based grading (SBG) or standards-based grading & reporting (SBGR):** A grading system where a subject is broken down into smaller goals and learning is assessed through each smaller target.
- **Social-emotional learning (SEL):** Social and emotional learning (SEL) includes the knowledge and skills needed to manage emotions and have positive relationships with others.
- **Science, Technology, Engineering, Arts, and Math (STEAM):** A common term that captures arts along with STEM subjects.
- **Science, Technology, Engineering, and Math (STEM):** A common catch-all term for all subjects that fall into these four categories.
- **Summative assessment:** An approach where student learning is evaluated at the end of a unit.
- **Third culture kids (TCKs):** A term used to describe the student population often prevalent within international schools. These students live in cultures outside of their home country and have many places in the world they may call home.
- **Tiers of international schools:** A phrase often used to describe the quality of an international school. Educators may refer to a school as a "Tier One" school. While there is no formal labeling of the international schools, some common indicators of "Tier One" schools may include accreditation, recognition by the U.S. Office of Overseas Schools, size of faculty, and type of curriculum.

Appendix A

- **Trailing spouse:** Used to describe a person who follows their partner to another country without having a position within the school.
- **Understanding by design (UBD):** A framework that offers a three-stage backward design process for curriculum planning and includes a template and set of design tools that embody the process.
- **Universal design for learning (UDL):** A method for learning and teaching that incorporates brain science to provide flexibility and the removal of obstacles so that all learners can succeed.
- **Workshop model:** Starts with a warm-up, a mini lesson, work time, and debrief session.

Institutional & Regional Organizations

Regional educational organizations serve as unifying entities that annually bring these international educators together to learn from one another and gain best practice. Some of these include:

- Association for the Advancement of International Education (AAIE)
- Association of American Schools in Central America, Colombia, the Caribbean and Mexico (The Tri-Association)
- Association of American Schools in South America (AASSA)
- Association of International Educators of Color (AIELOC)
- Association of International Schools in Africa (AISA)
- Academy for International School Heads (AISH)
- American International Schools in the Americas (AMISA)
- Association for Supervision and Curriculum Development (ASCD)
- Central and Eastern European Schools Association (CEESA)
- Council of International Schools (CIS)
- East Asia Regional Council of Schools (EARCOS)
- Educational Collaborative for International Students (ECIS)
- Mediterranean Association of International Schools (MAIS)
- Near East South Asia Council of Overseas Schools (NESA)

Appendix A

Accreditation

Accreditation serves as a mark of quality assurance within international schools and is provided by several U.S. regional associations and global agencies. Some of these include:

- Council of International Schools (CIS)
- Cognita
- International Council Advancing Independent School Accreditation (ICAISA)
- Middle States Association of Colleges and Schools (MSA)
- National Council for Private School Accreditation (NCPSA)
- New England Association of Schools and Colleges (NEASC)
- New York State Association of Independent Schools (NYSAIS)
- Southern Association of Independent Schools (SAIS)
- Western Association of Schools and Colleges (WASC)

References

Brown, G. C. (2000). Governing boards and U.S. interests. In R. Simpson & C. R. Duke (Eds.), *American overseas schools* (pp. 25–50). Phi Delta Kappa.

Bunnell, T. (2008). International education and the second phase: A framework for conceptualizing its nature and for the future of assessment of its effectiveness. *Compare, 38*(4), 414–426.

Waterson, M. (2016). The changing nature of the international school market. In M. C. Hayden & J. J. Thompson (Eds.), *International schools: Current issues and future prospects.* (pp. 185–213). Symposium Books.

Appendix B
International Recruiting Agencies

International schools actively recruit certified educators each year to fill positions within their schools due to their transient population. These positions can be highly sought after by educators throughout the world due to benefits, salary, and the opportunity to engage in developing an international global curriculum. Contracts generally require a two-year commitment which may include housing, tuition for dependents, and travel back and forth to their home country (country of origin or passport country). Some recruitment agencies include:

- Carney Sandoe (school leaders) – founded in 1977
- International Schools Services (school leaders and teachers) – founded in 1955
- RG-175 (school leaders) – founded in 2002
- Schrole (teachers) – founded in 2013
- Search Associates (school leaders and teachers) – founded in 1990
- Teach Away (teachers) – founded in 2003
- The International Educator – TIEOnline (teachers) – founded in 1986

Contributor Biographies

Philip Allen
Classroom Teacher, American School of Doha, Doha, Qatar
Phil has over 13 experience years working in international school settings in the Middle East and Southeast Asia. He has worked as a behavioral therapist and as a classroom teacher of various grades. Phil is a strong advocate for inclusion in international schools and recently completed his Masters in special education need and inclusion. Phil can be reached at pip_allen@hotmail.com.

Jamie Bacigalupo
High School English Teacher, Shekou International School, Shenzhen, China
Jamie began her international teaching career at 30 years old when she flew from her hometown of Minneapolis, Minnesota, to Quito, Ecuador. At the time, she was on a two-year sabbatical from her high school English position in Bloomington, Minnesota. Two years in Quito turned to three, as she let her position in the States be given to some other lovely Midwesterner. Her heart now belongs abroad. After teaching at Colegio Americano in Quito, Jamie accepted a position in Shenzhen, China. One month before accepting her position, while home for Christmas, she declared, "Mom, I would never move to the other side of the world. Never." She believes the universe chuckled and said, "Challenge accepted." Jamie can be reached at jnbacigalupo@gmail.com.

Laura Benson
Director of Curriculum and Professional Development, International Schools Services Centennial, Colorado USA
Laura Benson is the Director of Curriculum and Professional Development for International Schools Services and brings over 40 years of teaching

Contributor Biographies

and leadership experience to her work. She is the co-author of *Standards and Assessment: The Core of Quality Instruction* and *Bearing Witness* and published numerous articles in professional journals. Laura earned degrees from Trinity University and the University of Denver. A third culture child herself and international educator, Laura has lived and learned in China, the Netherlands, the Middle East, England, and over 90 countries of the world and hopes that borders can just become gates of friendship for all.

Lori Boll

Executive Director of SENIA, Bend, Oregon, USA
Lori Boll is an experienced special education leader with a personal connection to individuals with disabilities. In Shanghai, China, Lori co-founded the first inclusive school in the city. Lori also co-created and ran the Intensive Needs Program at IS Bangkok in 2017. Currently, she serves as SENIA International's Executive Director. She can be reached at lori@seniainternational.org.

Jay Brownrigg

Teacher, Yokohama International School, Yokohama, Japan
Jay has been an educator since 2005. Originally from Perth, Australia, he started teaching in local public secondary schools until he was offered a position as a primary school physical education teacher. From that point, he continued to excel in his subject area and then took the plunge to teach overseas. In 2010, Jay moved to Suzhou, China where he spent the next eight years of his life working in two great international schools in a variety of teaching and leadership positions. During his time in China, Jay got married and started a family. In 2018, his family moved from China to Yokohama, Japan. It is where he is working currently and thoroughly enjoys the lifestyle here. Jay can be contacted by email at jaydb81@gmail.com

Tsayli Lily Chang

Head of Early Years, Changchun American International School, Changchun, China
Tsayli Lily Chang is an educational leader with 15 years of classroom experience, born in Taipei, Taiwan, and grew up in New Jersey, United States. She has taught and lived in Taipei, Seoul, Abu Dhabi, Santiago, Shanghai, and currently in Changchun. She is happily married to her husband, who is also a fellow international educator, for the past 20 years.

Contributor Biographies

Elizabeth Heejin Cho

Principal of Teaching and Learning, Korea International School, South Korea
Liz Cho is passionate about empowering teachers and students. She currently calls San Diego, CA home in the U.S. though she grew up in Pittsburgh, PA, and taught in the Washington, DC area prior to teaching abroad. Internationally, Liz has worked at Shekou International School (SIS) and Gyeonggi Suwon International School (GSIS) before Korea International School (KIS). Liz's 13 years as a U.S. public school and an international school teacher before moving into administration full time in 2016 has taught her the value of a competent, empathic leader who models lifelong learning. Certified in Educational Technology, an ISTE Trainer, and an Apple Distinguished Educator, Liz is an avid believer in using innovative techniques to inspire educators through servant leadership. She also runs, silks, hoops, and has a horrible sense of direction. Any other professional information about Liz can be found at lizcho.org, and she can be reached at lizcho@me.com.

Sandra Chow

Director of Digital & Innovative Learning, Keystone Academy, Beijing, China
Sandra Chow is a veteran educator from Toronto, Canada and has taught in the Toronto District School Board, Morrison Academy Taipei, worked as an instructional liaison with TVO, and is currently at Keystone Academy in Beijing. She is a skilled and energetic educator passionate about innovation, educational technology, and expanding the horizons of education. She is an Apple Distinguished Educator, Google Certified Innovator, Google Certified Trainer, Microsoft Innovative Educator Expert, and a Google Earth Education Expert Leader. Her experience as a professional accountant, a cross-cultural educator, and a networker provides her with a unique perspective as a leader. She strives to prepare students and train educators to learn, teach, collaborate, and create in a globally competitive society. Sandra can be reached at www.classroomdollop.com and via email at watnunu@gmail.com

Monika Dewan, Ph.D.

Advisor, Khaitan Public School, Ghaziabad, India
CEO, Adarsh Educational Solutions, New Delhi, India
Monika Dewan, Ph.D. has been an international educator, author, and advisor in physical and health education for more than two decades. She

Contributor Biographies

specializes in training for life skills, mindfulness, communication skills, program assessment, and curriculum development. Monika has 25 years of rich experience as an advisor and an educator. She has taught and has been the director of the summer program at the American Embassy School (AES) in New Delhi for more than two decades. She has also taught at Delhi University and at an Indian school. She believes that learning is a lifelong process. Monika recently launched a company named Adarsh Educational Solutions. Follow her on Instagram @adarsheducationalsolutions and on LinkedIn @drmonikadewan. Her email address is: monikadewan9@gmail.com

Sally Edwards
English Teacher, Oegstgeest, The Netherlands
Sally is an English teacher who was born and educated on the South coast of England. She teaches English at a Montessori primary school in Oegstgeest, near The Hague in The Netherlands. Sally runs her own business as a private tutor to primary school children and also produce and write podcasts and blogs about mindfulness. Sally can be reached at sally_edwards2002@yahoo.com.

Beccy Fox
Head of School, Think International School, Hong Kong
Beccy has worked in schools since 1989 and took up her first overseas position at the International School Seychelles in 1998. Since then she has worked in schools in Malaysia and Indonesia. She is currently a headteacher at an international school in Hong Kong. Becky's original home was Essex in England, but since getting married and having a child, she now calls Bali her home.

David Han
MYP Mathematics and Schoolwide Academics, Seoul Foreign School, Seoul, South Korea
Born in Seoul, South Korea, raised in Los Angeles, California, David attended UCLA as an undergrad and Loyola Marymount University for graduate studies. He has taught physical education, computers, elementary school math, middle school math & science, language arts, and religion. He served as an athletic director and assistant principal at St. Anastasia School in Westchester, California prior to moving to American International School in Hong Kong as an Elementary School Assistant Principal. Currently, David

Contributor Biographies

teaches high school mathematics at Seoul Foreign School in Seoul, South Korea. You can find him on Twitter: @mrdavehan

Erika Hardy
Learning Support Specialist, American School of Guatemala, Guatemala City, Guatemala
Erika was born and raised in Albuquerque, New Mexico. She completed her bachelor's degree in strategic communication at the University of New Mexico and her master's degree in special education at Grand Canyon University. She left Albuquerque and found her way to Dallas, Texas where she began her first role as a classroom teacher. After leaving Texas, she embarked on her international teaching journey at the American School of Guatemala in Guatemala City, Guatemala, where she has spent the past five years. Erika can be reached at erika.hardyy@hotmail.com.

Mick Hill
NHL-Stenden, International Teacher Education for Primary School, Meppel, The Netherlands
Mick Hill is a Dutch and British national who grew up in The Netherlands. Before finding his passion for teaching, he was a struggling student that went to practical education and became an assistant nurse. As part of this program, he got placed in a primary school and found his calling. During his teacher education, Mick gained international teaching experiences in five different countries, with five different curricula, and specialized in inclusive education, mathematics, and outdoor and physical education. Mick can be reached at mickandrewjack@gmail.com.

David Lovelin, EdD
High School Principal, Hong Kong International School, Hong Kong, Tai Tam
Dr. David Lovelin has been an administrator for the past 17 years in several different roles and is currently the high school principal for Hong Kong International School. Previously, David worked at Korea International School (KIS) and in the United States at Sam Barlow High School, Lake Oswego High School, and Woodrow Wilson High School in varied leadership roles. David is committed to developing innovative

Contributor Biographies

education programs, promoting a positive culture, building relationships, and grounded in supporting all learners. David can be contacted at davejlovelin@gmail.com

Ann Marie Luce
Head of School, Kehoe-France Southshore, Metairie, Louisiana
Dr. Ann Marie is a scholar-practitioner from London, Ontario, Canada. As an international educator, Ann Marie has served various school communities in London, Ontario, Canada, China, Denmark, and the United States. Ann Marie completed her educational doctorate at Gonzaga University, where her research focused on leadership cultural intelligence. She is currently the head of school at Kehoe-France Southshore in Metairie, Louisiana in the United States. Ann Marie can be reached at aluce@kehoe-france.com.

Alex Munro
MYP Individual & Societies Teacher, NIST International School Bangkok, Bangkok, Thailand
Alex is originally from the D.C metropolitan area. He has been in education for five years. He began as a special education assistant in Chicago, Illinois (LaSalle Language Academy). After a couple of years there, Alex decided to teach abroad in Bangkok, Thailand (KPIS International School). Since being abroad, he has worked at two international schools in Bangkok. You can find him on Twitter: @BaMunro21

Elizabeth Ochieng Onayemi
Senior School English Teacher, International School of Uganda, Kampala, Uganda
Elizabeth is originally from Kenya where she trained as a teacher. She has previously taught at Number 4 High School of Baotou, Inner Mongolia China, the International College of the Hunan Agricultural University in Changsha, Hunan Province China, Miras International School in Astana, Kazakhstan, and the International Programs School (IPS) in Saudi Arabia. Elizabeth is currently employed at the International School of Uganda. She can be reached at eochieng1@gmail.com.

Contributor Biographies

Nicolas Pavlos
Head of Visual & Performing Arts, American School of Warsaw, Warsaw, Poland
Born in Warsaw, Poland, Nicolas teaches theatre/drama at the same international school his father once led as director. Joining the family business (as an international teacher) was career number two, though he has no doubt that his love of performing and acting was born of his many moves across many continents. Nicolas can be reached via email at bnomadic@gmail.com.

Brenda Perkins
Lower School Counselor, Taipei American School, Taipei, Taiwan
Brenda has lived and worked in international school communities for over 25 years. Her professional experiences range from science teaching to wellness education and curriculum, and currently school counseling. Brenda is a certified mindfulness teacher and is passionate about mental health and well-being in schools. Brenda can be reached at brenda.perkins.101@gmail.com.

Kelly Anne Scotti
IBDP Coordinator, English Language and Literature Teacher, American International School of Johannesburg, Johannesburg, South Africa
Kelly is originally from Windsor, Ontario, Canada where she taught high school English before moving abroad. She has served in many roles in Hong Kong, Germany, China, Cambodia, and South Africa. Kelly can be reached at kelly_scotti@yahoo.ca.

Rebecca F. Stallworth
Itinerant School Counselor, Bering Strait School District, Unakaleet, Alaska, USA
Rebecca is an educator with 14 years of experience in PK-12 and mainly worked in rural schools in West Alabama. During those summers, she worked with high school students who were part of a summer enrichment program at a higher education institution. Her international experience started as a study abroad student in England during her sophomore year

in college. Her need to live abroad was reinvigorated to the point that she decided to live and work abroad after working in the States for 11 years. Her email is stall027@crimson.ua.edu.

Cheryl-Ann Weekes
High School Counselor, International Community School of Abidjan, Abidjan, Ivory Coast
After working for 13 years in the U.S., in 2010 Cheryl-Ann started a journey as an international school counselor. She planned to stay one year, but soon realized that she would have a better work life-balance working in international schools. She has lived and worked in the Dominican Republic, Jamaica, Ethiopia, Thailand, Egypt, and now in the Ivory Coast. She can be reached at crweekes7@gmail.com.

Printed in the United States
by Baker & Taylor Publisher Services